D0908916

JOHN STRACHAN

CANADIAN BIOGRAPHICAL STUDIES

UNIVERSITY OF TORONTO PRESS

J. L. H. HENDERSON

John Strachan

1778-1867

© University of Toronto Press 1969

Printed in Canada

SBN 8020 3225 7

The *Canadian Biographical Studies* is allied with the project of the *Dictionary of Canadian Biography/Dictionnaire biographique du Canada.*

These small volumes are designed primarily to interest the general reader, and they will be published in two languages. They seek to fill a gap in our knowledge of secondary figures, often non-political figures of regional and national importance in Canada's past.

In these *Studies*, the emphasis is upon an interpretation rather than a life. The limitation in size challenges the author to consider the best use of anecdote, description of place, reference to general history, and use of quotation. The general reader will be offered the fruits of recent research. Not all of the volumes will aim at full comprehensiveness and completeness: some may be followed later by larger and fuller studies of the subject. Many of the present studies, it is hoped, may suggest new interpretive possibilities not only about the central figure but about his period.

The editors have not followed two of Plutarch's chief standards: the subjects of these *Studies* have not been chosen only for their public virtue, or for their acknowledged distinction. Most of them lived out their lives in Canada, but for some their careers were conducted partly in other theatres. Some have been chosen because, though they were once widely known, they have since been undeservedly neglected. Some have been selected not for their obvious leadership or eminence, but because they were sufficiently prominent to represent some of the qualities that guided their age, men of significance if not of first prominence.

Some have been grouped in studies that should throw light on interesting families, professional groups, or lobbies in our past.

Thus, the *Studies* is not one of biography alone, but of social, economic and political history approached through the careers and ideas – acknowledged, but often unrecognized – of Canadians of many ranks and diverse times.

ALAN WILSON

Contents

I am aware that Scots must be called Scots. John Strachan didn't know it. To him, the inhabitants of North Britain were either Scotch or Highlandmen. Settlers who came to America from the British Isles were Emigrants. Only an American would invent the concept Immigrant. In British America, Canadian was reserved for the French-speaking. The others were British or American, or if long settled, British Americans. Upper Canadian was a growing possibility. There were, of course, no Anglicans. That was a Latinism. There were Churchmen, English Churchmen or members of the Scotch Church or Kirk. There were also dissenters, Presbyterian, Methodist, Tunker, and the like. Americans or Scotch in communion with the English Church were called Episcopals or Episcopalians, an unsatisfactory name that yet might also be applied to Churchmen in Upper Canada.

J.L.H.H.

JOHN STRACHAN

Schoolmaster and Minister

In 1785 when John was seven, the Strachan family held a council. Mrs. Strachan advanced the proposition that her youngest son should be educated for a minister. Her husband, John Strachan the quarrier, objected. The idea was not sensible, and her supporting evidence was less so, that he had been born at noon on the Sunday, at high tide, when the sacrament was being dispensed in the parish church of Aberdeen. The family had done well since moving into the city from Glenbucket on Donside. Mr. Strachan was overseer in the quarry, doing the steady, responsible, outdoor work he preferred. The girls, Margaret, twenty, and Rachel, eighteen, were safely reared and about to be on their own. The older boys, James, twelve, and William, ten, were apprenticed to respectable trades. The next step was to provide for the young boy, to pay the premiums of an apprenticeship and start him on his way. No one known to John Strachan possessed the influence that would give his son a church, supposing that he should proceed so far, nor did he know of any class more pitiable than the unemployed would-be minister. As the family council continued, it seemed clear that Mrs. Strachan's proposal was impossible. Then James, the eldest son, cast in his vote with his mother's, and a compromise was agreed upon. The boy would go to the "Latin," the Aberdeen Grammar School, for one or two years.

Obediently, John Strachan the younger worked his way through Aberdeen Grammar as year followed year. Afterwards he accounted it one of the happiest days of his life when he made the top position in the beginner's class, despite a late start in term, but it was not a position he could maintain. More memorable in a schoolboy world was his being chosen to pick the apples in the rector's walled garden, into which even

Dr. Dun's servants were not allowed. He was early useful to persons in authority. After grammar school must come university. His father refused to contribute further to the lost cause of education. Young John applied for, and won, a bursary at King's College up in the old town of Aberdeen, deciding that though Marischal College was closer, its bursaries gave precedence to the sons of burghers. For the five winter months he walked to that ancient crowned tower each day and completed the first of the four terms.

Then disaster struck. The elder Strachan was hit in the eye by a splinter of granite when a delayed charge exploded, and after eight days died. John Strachan must now continue on his own, and to some degree contribute to the support of his mother. He was sixteen, and it was too late to seek a trade or to pay the premium to enter. An experience that summer pointed up his predicament and the perils attached to education. As soon as he had buried his father he went up to Banff to enter the service of Lady Harriet Gordon as tutor to her grandchildren. It was a recognized form of employment for Scotch university men, and many a would-be minister had endured it before Strachan, teaching in a family until school or manse turned up, hoping for the influence of the family to secure the one or the other. The position always had its anomalies. You were half professional, and half servant. Lady Harriet can be forgiven if she looked upon this rough young man as a convenient nursery maid and an object of compassion. Strachan was outraged at the threat to his independence. On the first morning she offered him tea or porridge for breakfast. "Tea, certainly," he replied. "When I wish for porrage I shall ask them."[1] Oats to a Scotchman were

1   Trinity College, Toronto, Manuscript relic.

always a plural, and porridge and the humbles pie he ate in that noble household were not what Strachan considered the due of education.

For the summer after his second term he was able to secure a school at Cannonside in Angus. After the third year he won the appointment to the parish school at Denino (Dunino) in Fife. These, with modest sums gained by coaching in term, saw him through. He was graduated Master of Arts in March of 1796 aware that though his education was negligible, the way to the professions was now open.

The next step towards his mother's goal of hearing him preach took him to St. Andrews. In the Faculty of Divinity in that university full-time students could be graduated after three years' study. "Partial attenders" could hope to finish in six. Strachan was parish schoolmaster at Denino, only four miles outside the city. It had paid for his last year at King's. It now permitted his registration and occasional attendance in divinity. For a few brief months, in that ruined old ecclesiastical capital, he revelled in the company of other graduate students. In his own eyes "the merry dominie of Denino," he began what were to be lifelong friendships with Thomas Duncan and Thomas Chalmers, debated with John Campbell, the later lord chancellor, and urged upon him migration to the English bar. Regrettably he also fell in love, with a Denino girl. There was nothing he could do. Unable to hope for marriage or to declare his passion, he moved, obtaining the parish school of Kettle (King's Kettle), larger and worth fifty pounds a year, but deep in Fife and too far to continue even partial attendance at St. Andrews.

The young schoolmaster was now at something of an impasse. It would be pleasant to record that his mother's vision was justified – that he was demonstrably the most pious, the most brilliant, or the most promising graduate of King's College and that Scotland waited upon him. He was none of these things. Virtue, hard work, and independence of spirit must be their own rewards. His father had been in the right, of course. Scotland had a surfeit of busy young men aiming at the professions. Patronage or family connections were necessary to secure a lodgement. The alternatives were emigration or the old journey south to London.

Strachan twice secured a patron. Dr. James Beattie, professor of moral philosophy at Marischal College, had been responsible for his summer with Lady Harriet Gordon. His son Montagu was Strachan's bosom friend as an undergraduate. And Dr. Beattie was a lion indeed, friend of Dr. Samuel Johnson and of the Bishop of London, author of *The Minstrel* and of a celebrated *Essay on Truth*. Unfortunately young Montagu died and Dr. Beattie, approached soon after for a recommendation for a position, refused, and Strachan knew himself to be turned off. Denino provided a second and more agreeable patron in the person of James Brown, minister of the parish. Dr. Brown had been a professor at St. Andrews and Denino was a college living. In 1795 he had accepted appointment as professor of natural philosophy at the University of Glasgow. A large, cultivated, questioning bachelor in his thirties, he was to prove a lifelong influence upon the younger man, but in 1796 Brown occasioned some agonizing decisions. In Glasgow he was nervously incapacitated from carrying on his lectures after the first term. He sought an assistant, offered the post to Strachan, then reconsidered and retired on a pension. For a few tantalizing weeks Strachan saw a university career stretching ahead of him in his favourite field of natural philosophy, and the memory of that delightful prospect plagued him for years. Any post in a university, however humble, must be satisfying in itself and lead on to greater things. Instead he returned to the steady drudgery of being a parish schoolmaster.

Release, when it came, was emigration with a difference. Two merchants in British North America, Richard Cartwright and Robert Hamilton, wanted a schoolmaster for their children. They offered a contract for three years at eighty pounds a year, with passage paid. Dr. James Brown passed on the offer, and John Strachan debated within himself and then accepted. There was some suggestion of a government-sponsored grammar school being set up and, more vaguely, mention of an academy or college. These possibilities were to look large in retrospect, but they were not fixed items in any engagement the merchants could offer, nor were they necessary. "My curiosity to see foreign parts, my ignorance of the country, the small appearance I then had of soon obtaining a Church, with many other reasons still more frivolous, determined me."[2] America would be a three-year interruption in his career, a source of interest and of profit. He called on his mother, finding her strangely fearful and dissuasive, travelled back and forth across Scotland seeing his friends, and took ship from Greenock on August 25, 1799. To Brown he wrote: "When you read this I am on the Atlantic. My departure is not embittered by any patriotic feelings, yet tho' I leave my country with the greatest indifference. I leave my friends with the most sincere regret. I go by way of New York which is perhaps of advantage as I shall endeavour to secure a retreat *there* in case my

2   *Ibid.*

situation should prove disagreeable. ... My aim shall always be to preserve my independence."[3]

Richard Cartwright, merchant and forwarder, of Kingston, Upper Canada, was a large and formidable man. He fled Albany in the province of New York in the early days of the revolution and had established himself at the outflow of Lake Ontario even before government had brought up loyalists to settle Kingston and the five townships beyond. A cast in one eye marred his countenance and conceivably increased the reserve with which he looked out upon his world. If the revolution had not intervened he would have proceeded to holy orders in the Church of England, and his love of books and his prodigious memory were objects of wonder. His close friend was the Reverend John Stuart, six foot and ramrod straight, the missionary in Kingston. When Stuart's son, George Okill, had left for Harvard College for his degree, the town school he had taught closed. Cartwright, his own sons' education at a standstill, had sent to Scotland for a tutor. As a member of the Legislative Council of the province he knew the hopelessness of any plans for state education. With his sometime partner, Robert Hamilton of Queenston, he simply made his own arrangements. The details survive among his business accounts, the first disappointments, and then success. "The two eldest share in my impatience and anxiety to see Mr. Strachan."[4]

On the last night of the year 1799 John Strachan drove into Kingston by sleigh from Montreal. He sent a note around to Cartwright's house and, being summoned, went and supped and stayed.

The three years that followed were for Strachan something of a holi-

3 Ontario Department of Public Records and Archives (henceforth PAO), Strachan Papers, Strachan to Brown, 25 Aug. 1799.
4 Queen's University, Kingston, Richard Cartwright Papers.

day. It is true that he had duties and went daily from his study in Cartwright's house to the schoolroom in town, but there were only a dozen
boys to be taught, and one girl, Cartwright's Hannah, and they made a
very domestic academy indeed. The children ranged so widely in age
that each had to be instructed separately, the negligent and philosophical Andrew Stuart, the diverse Cartwrights, Dic and James, the Hamil-
tons, and after a few months, John Beverley Robinson, a grave and
stately ten-year-old, protégé of the missionary. John Strachan had signed
a contract which he would not break, and for three years his career must
be postponed while he enjoyed this pleasant company.

The principal disability was the absence of like-minded persons of
his own age, the cheerful and disputatious company of Scotch university men he was used to, and in letters home he called it a dull life. Short
trips to Montreal were occasionally possible and dinners with the
McGills or the Frobishers or the sundry Scotch who made up that mer-
cantile society, but such delights were rare. He made an early voyage
up-water to Queenston and Niagara Falls, but hesitated to repeat it. He
suffered from seasickness at the beginning of every voyage, so the lake
at his door was no call to adventure. The feeling of being upon a frontier
was wasted upon him. Bears on the road, deer straying into town,
roused in him no urge to hunt. He knew himself to be an intellectual,
educated at some cost to himself, and he took pains not to lose his
identity. An autobiography[5] written that first winter may be an exercise
in egotism but it closely and honestly explored the way he had come,
the people he knew, and, without undue introversion, the person he was.
He would not be lost in this wilderness, even to himself.

5   Trinity College, Manuscript relic.

From autobiography he turned to verse, Scots verse first as became a man who always whistled Scots, then translations from the classics, and at last playful rhymes in English, corrected by Cartwright, for the boys to read at school, or even for ladies to read when alone. For once more, in this holiday time, John Strachan fell in love. The girl was Margaret England, a secure young woman a few months older than himself, sister to one of his schoolboys. Nothing could come of it, for he had early arranged with Mr. Cartwright to send half of his salary home twice a year, but Strachan enjoyed being gallant to women, and the urge to make marriage possible began to enter into his forming plans.

His intention, of course, was to return home and resume his studies. He had scouted the opportunities in New York on his way up. He was learning French in case there was good cause for delay on the way back, but St. Andrews was the acknowledged goal. Then, in the fall of 1802, he took steps that would cancel all his earlier plans. He sought to have himself ordained for a colonial parish. Cartwright was his adviser, but one suspects Miss England of being the inspiration. Hearing that Gabriel Street Presbyterian Church in Montreal might become vacant, he wrote suggesting himself for the office.[6] There was no vacancy, but almost simultaneously, through John Stuart, he offered himself for a church under government. Whatever Strachan's motives, Cartwright and Stuart knew their man, and the needs of the church. The recruit was sent on a brief missionary journey downriver to New Oswegatchie while arrangements went forward. In March 1803 he was nominated by the Lieutenant Governor to the newly vacant parish of Cornwall. That spring he

6   Queen's University, Kingston, William Morris Papers, Strachan to Blackwood, 20 Aug. and 21 Sept. 1802.

received the sacrament for the first time in his life, in St. George's Church, Kingston, at the hands of John Stuart. In May he went down to Quebec to meet the bishop and to be ordained.

The Reverend John Strachan faced his first congregation and preached his first sermon in June of 1803, and was surprised at his own diffidence. For the immediate problem of living, he took over an abandoned log cabin and repaired it with the help of the boy John Robinson. Miss England married someone else that July, so life was spared that complication though Strachan was outraged at being jilted.

Cornwall was one more of the riverside villages settled by loyalist refugees in 1784. Such importance as it had was occasioned by the rapids in the river, which here again forced trans-shipment of goods and people in the long supply line from Montreal to the lakes. Strachan in describing the place to Brown could say: "My flock is not numerous. A great part of my parish belongs to the Lutheran persuasion, a greater has no religion at all. A number of the people are Catholics, and plenty of Presbyterians with a few Methodists. You see I am in a pickle."[7]

A "pickle" is a cheerful way to describe it. By taking orders in the colonial church Strachan had cut himself off from both Scotland and England. The Scotch had no place for men in English orders. England denied the right of presentation to livings to men ordained outside. He was now a clergyman for the colonies only, or for the United States or Ireland, and his mother would never hear him preach. A later age was to see in his ordination by a bishop a turning from Presbyterianism to Anglicanism, and a change not dictated by conscience, as John Stuart's had been, but by convenience. The "conversion" was indeed a matter

7   Strachan Papers, Strachan to Brown, 27 Oct. 1803.

of anxious thought and of reference back to his mother and his friends in Scotland (who approved). But when it came down to it, the two establishments of Scotland and England were much alike. They were not competitors. Each considered itself secure within its own half of the kingdom. Theological differences were at their lowest point. Migration involved change. More important to this holidaying schoolmaster was the fact that he was exchanging Britain and the life he knew for a career in this colony.

Now that the decision had been taken, the relatively idle years were over. Strachan set to work with energy and common sense. The parish had to be made and he would do it well. A church was built, a wooden oblong with proper windows, a bell tower with a bell, a spire on top of the tower coated with tin and visible up and down the river, and a weather-vane above that for wayfarers to consult, the best church in the province. The pews were sold to pay the cost of the building, with free sittings reserved for the poor, and shortly a gallery was added for the overflow. He gave himself to the study of theology. Sermons were written out on Saturday nights, written straight through without other aids than the Bible, preached as written, and then listed in the same book he had once used for college debates. From the beginning they were practical sermons, aimed at the mixed congregation he set about to collect. One missionary journey he made that summer, up to Augusta township, the old Oswegatchie, where he reported the continuing need for a mission station. He was not to be a travelling missionary however. In the fall a school would begin.

Cornwall Grammar School was opened for the sake of the boys he had taught in Kingston but it would not be a domestic academy as Kingston had been. The school would be his own, the methods and sole direction his, the costs his and the profits. He built a proper schoolhouse near the church, the windows sensibly above eye level to avoid distractions. Quickly he had not only the best school in the colony, for there were few contenders, but a demonstration of what a school could be. His boys would be grounded in the classics, ready in composition and debate, aware of the new studies growing out of natural philosophy, versed in all practical aids to making their way in the Canadas. Strachan was fortunate in his pupils. Sons of the leading emigrants, they were bound to become the colonial élite, the merchants, the legislators, the judiciary. Cornwall called forth their brains, pooled their ideas and associations, and gave them a cohesion that was the first real tie binding those whom men came to call the "family compact." It was a good school. When the legislature made provision to support eight district grammar schools, Strachan's was named that for the Eastern District, without change in its circumstances other than the addition of a hundred pounds a year salary for the schoolmaster. Strachan's clear intent was to use his "academy" as the basis for a colonial college when the opportunity should offer.

And if his life was now committed to Upper Canada, it might as well be pleasant. He built a parsonage house, the first in the province, with garden and offices, and he married a Cornwall girl.

Ann Wood McGill at twenty-two was already a widow. At eighteen she had married the Montreal merchant, Andrew McGill, and on his premature death had returned home. A gentle, pretty person with a flair for neatness and a readiness to be hospitable, Strachan was charmed with her then and remained charmed for fifty years. It was as well. At the annual examinations for the school forty guests sat down to dinner. One boy, at least, always lived with the schoolmaster. Another wrote home: "He lives in great style and keeps three servants. He is a great friend to the poor and spends his money as fast as he gets it."[8] Money was certainly no longer a problem. Two hundred pounds came to him as missionary, three hundred from the school in fees and salary. His wife had three hundred more in lieu of any claims upon the McGill estate. There was enough to spare for relatives in Aberdeen, for the school, and for the parsonage, and enough to begin and to provide for that most delightful of creations, a family of one's own. James McGill Strachan, Mary Elizabeth, and George were born in the Cornwall parsonage.

Finally there were books to be written. Strachan was never long without some projected volume on his desk. Much of the writing arose from the needs of the school. An arithmetic textbook was written and published in Montreal because nothing available quite suited Upper Canada. Poems and essays for use in school also found their way into print, many of them under the pseudonym of "The Reckoner" in the new *Kingston Gazette*. Some few of the seventy columns contributed to that weekly suggested that another frontier humorist and observer of colonial ways was developing, but the mood was not sustained, and moral essays took over. Two works were published for the sake of the school in a special sense: *The Christian religion, recommended in a Letter to his Pupils* and *A Discourse on the character of King George the third.*[9]

8   PAO, Ridout Papers, George Ridout to Samuel Ridout, 24 June 1807.
9   Montreal: Nahum Mower, 1807 and 1810 respectively.

They indicated that at Cornwall boys were taught loyalty to church and king, and as one consequence in 1811 the University of King's College, Aberdeen, conferred upon its graduate the degree of doctor of divinity.

The years at Cornwall might have followed one another without change until death came, for colonial clergy often lived and died in their one parish. Strachan could speculate how he and his school might grow greater or be moved elsewhere. There were few possibilities of either.

The proposal to found a college in Montreal was made in Cornwall parsonage house in February 1811. James McGill was spending a week with his former sister-in-law and her husband. By Strachan's account, "the conversation frequently turned upon the want of an English seminary of education. ... Mr. McGill, feeling the infirmities of old age fast approaching, the conversation at times took a serious turn and comprised remarks upon the disposition of his property which was very considerable, for he had neither children nor any near relations." His host suggested that he leave his money after his death for the education of youth. "It would be doing something to the glory of God and hand down his name with praise to posterity." In consequence, McGill "relished the hint so well that he was continually dwelling upon it – he wished the matter put in some sort of form and expressed a determination to establish a College in his lifetime on condition that I would remove to Montreal, become principal, and take upon me the superintendance [sic]."[10]

Thus prompted, McGill made his will. Strachan's eldest child, McGill's namesake, was to receive 1380 acres of land. The bulk of the

10 Archives of the United Society for the Propagation of the Gospel, London (SPGA), Strachan to the Secretary, 17 April 1824.

estate, £10,000 currency and the house and grounds called Burnside, was to be turned over to four trustees, including Strachan, for conveyance to the Royal Institution for the Advancement of Learning, on the condition that they establish a college and grammar schools within ten years. McGill died the nineteenth of December in 1813, in the midst of war, but the first step at least had been taken to begin a university.

John Stuart also died in Kingston; loss as it was, the death opened up that pleasant parish, the perfect site for a good school. Strachan hoped to succeed him, but had to give way as soon as Stuart's widow intimated that she would like her son George Okill to have the succession and with it the office of bishop's commissary or agent for the upper colony. There remained the possibility that he would take George Stuart's far-from-thriving mission of York, but he refused. York was an inferior village cursed with petty politics. Sir Francis Gore, the lieutenant governor, stopping off in Cornwall on his way home on leave, urged him to go. Isaac Brock, administrator in Gore's stead, offered the additional post of chaplain to the garrison and an additional salary, and Strachan was persuaded. Late in June 1812 he came with his family to York.

John Strachan arrived in York at the same time that war came again to British North America. That war was to bring the missionary and schoolmaster to a prominence he had not known before.

In the minds of the British, the American declaration of war in 1812 was one more complication in the wars against Napoleon, a consequence of the blockade of Europe and a distraction to be settled when ships and troops were available. If diplomacy and moderation would serve instead of battle, then time was gained. The weak point was Upper Canada. Designed by nature to be part of the old American northwest, it lay open to any invasion, impossible to hold against an enemy in control of the lakes. The inhabitants had little to gain by a defensive war except the problematical retention of British sovereignty, and who could tell how many preferred that to American union. The sensible course for Upper Canadians was to sit quietly and to leave the issue to the arbitrament of arms elsewhere.

Years before in Denino, John Strachan had joined in resistance to the creation of a Scotch militia in the face of a threatened invasion of Britain. Government had required that the schoolmasters list the eligible males in each parish, and he had not complied. The scare soon passed, public opinion was against a compulsory militia, and he suffered no ill consequences save having to convince a board of heritors that he was not as democratic as they feared. Now in York, Upper Canada, he behaved entirely differently. One is tempted to smile at how thoroughly his loyalist pupils had educated him, or at the effect of years and authority. In fact he was now an interested party. He had a stake in this country such as he had never had in Scotland. These settlements in the interior of a continent held the promise of growing into a new and interesting British nation, "our liberty giving our country the most solid charms, notwithstanding its freezing sky and procrastinated snows."[11] The Americans, in his view, saw the matter rightly. They would eliminate Upper Canada before it posed a threat to the takeover of the continent. The French could be ignored. The maritime colonies could ripen and fall at their leisure. The upper province must be taken, its rich

11 John Strachan, *A Discourse on the character of King George the third* (Montreal: Mower, 1810), p. 41.

crown lands and clergy reserves parcelled out to American settlers, and after a few years' peaceful possession there could be no return. He had adopted the Upper Canadian loyalist attitude in its entirety.

Dr. Strachan therefore fought his War of 1812 on two fronts. The duty of resistance to the invaders, in a Christian but determined fashion, was the burden of his preaching before the legislature in July and of his every public utterance and act thereafter. His private and public letters bristle against the British policy of appeasement, against the abortive armistice in the fall of 1812, against British governors who avoided war and commanders who avoided action. This land he had adopted must be held.

York was at first spared actual hostilities. Armies and irregulars came in over the borders at Sandwich and on the Niagara river. York was simply the civil capital, a staging area for the military, a base hospital for the wounded. Strachan's duties confined him to the town. He taught school daily, officiated on Sundays in the church, visited the hospitals. With others, he organized the Loyal and Patriotic Society of Upper Canada which gathered funds, supplied comforts for the militia, and rather grandly contemplated a series of medals for valour. As parson, he offered prayers over the flags the ladies presented to the militia companies, he prayed and spoke in every ward of the hospitals, and he buried those who died. Unhappily his own daughter fell sick of the ague from the Don marshes and in that first September died, "a sweet infant, exceedingly interesting."

In the late fall the government laid down the keel of a ship beside the bay, the *Sir Isaac Brock,* and York became at once a prime target for attack. Throughout the winter, men, women and children watched her grow, debating whether she would be completed and able to sail off to join the fleet in Kingston. The spring break-up came early, and soon after came the American fleet laden with troops for the Niagara frontier but prepared first to dispose of the *Brock*. The sails of the ships filing in past Gibraltar Point were handsome to behold. General Sheaffe, the administrator, who happened to be in York, did the strategic thing. He kept the militia out of battle, fought a short delaying action with provincial troops, blew up the magazine, arranged for the burning of the uncompleted *Brock*, and moved his precious regulars out onto the road for Kingston. William Allan, storekeeper, churchwarden, and major in the militia, was left to arrange the capitulation. Strachan joined himself to Allan in a furious round of activity, but it is questionable whether his rage was occasioned more by the Americans or by the English. He helped write the capitulation, objected when its signing was delayed, objected when he thought its terms were disregarded. He argued with junior officers and bullied General Dearborn. He tried to bully a private soldier and had a musket presented to his chest, forgetting that while generals might be amenable to civil control, privates are not. More proper to his office, he rescued Angelique Givins and her brood from looters while Major Givins led the Indians resisting the landing, and he arranged that the militiamen who had capitulated be fed. In the end he had nothing but praise for American officers and one became his house guest. Various Upper Canadians were more dangerous than the invaders, as they sought to work off old scores. Commodore Chauncey was of the opinion that he had never known a town with so many traitors in it. When the wind permitted, the fleet sailed out of the bay for its military objectives on the Niagara.

The first capture of York established the pattern. On July 31 Isaac Chauncey called again in force, and this time Strachan and Dr. Grant Powell were the reception committee, rowing out to the fleet with a white flag held high and exchanging courtesies on the flagship. The commodore, with many apologies, agreed to return the town's looted private library while York militiamen used the time to hide public stores up the Don.

That September of 1813, Jacob Mountain, Bishop of Quebec, came up to York, bewigged, gentlemanly, sitting in an armchair in a canoe paddled by eight Indians. The ordinances of the church must continue despite war and invasion, and Strachan took satisfaction in presenting in this his first confirmation class in York, a pair of ensigns and a midshipman on parole, Angelique Givins and her eldest, Mrs. Grant Powell, and the usual young people in suitable numbers.

There was one ironical consequence to the bishop's visit. Strachan reasoned that York could now be taken at will by the Americans and that Britain was prepared to give up everything above Kingston. The lands bordering Lake Erie and the Detroit had fallen. The front lines were drawn back to Burlington and further retreat seemed likely. If the bishop could travel without escort to York, Ann Strachan, six months pregnant again, could be got away to the safety of Cornwall and her mother's home. He sent her off, therefore, with her brother and the children and the servants in a bateau. She reached Cornwall safely. So, a fortnight later, did ten thousand American soldiers, for this was the attack on Montreal that was scotched at Crysler's Farm. The second Elizabeth Strachan was born in Cornwall in January 1814 but not before her father had obtained leave from government and hastened down overland through the snow, by sleigh and saddle horse, to strengthen his nervously prostrated wife.

The war stopped late in 1814, but the attitudes it had aroused were to remain. British regiments had held the low ridge at Lundy's Lane through a long summer night with the roar of Niagara in their ears. British American militia had fought beside them. The colony would be more consciously British hereafter. British emigrants would come out and take up the empty land. English institutions would be reinforced, and the American would be suspect on his own frontier.

No man emerged from the war more ready to play his part in the new order than John Strachan. He had shown himself resolute and responsible. He had given leadership at awkward moments. He had earned the respect and friendship of administrators. He would now see that this restored colony would live up to the promise inherent in its constitution and its fertile land. What his exact role would be was, in 1815, a matter of some speculation. Three separate careers were possible. He could devote himself principally to education, or to the church, or to government. He could coax a unified school system into being and cap it with a university, and this was presumably his first love. Or he could work for the increase of the church, its clergy and its missions, and, with luck and the right connections, be appointed its bishop. Or he could become a member of the legislature or the executive or both and govern the country. In fact no choice had to be made, since all could be combined.

As missionary in York and master of the Home District Grammar School he was already entered upon two of these careers. He now sought and accepted membership on the councils. Strachan knew that he had what the Scotch called "an aptitude for affairs." He could be busy here at the centre of things. The fact that he was, and knew himself to be, blunt and direct of speech, of strong feelings, pertinacious, and if need be devious, would ensure that life at the centre would be interesting.

First, though, John Strachan had to become a householder. York had no parsonage, nor had the war years been propitious for building, so he had lived in a rented house. Returning one March day in 1815 from visiting the military hospital he found his home in flames. Ann, pregnant again with the third son John, was safe at a neighbour's, and helpful passers-by were flinging books and furniture out of the upstairs window. It was the usual trouble with such houses, flame creeping from a faulty chimney into the woodwork, and Strachan counted himself fortunate that it had happened by day. He moved into one of Cartwright's properties (and suffered another fire there within two years) while a permanent house could be built. He chose a site out on Front Street, east of the town and facing the bay. The house was to be of brick, the first use of the material for a purely private residence, and it would have all the marks of permanence and stability: strong chimneys, a study, drawing-rooms, jalousies against the sun, a semicircular carriage way, room and to spare for a growing family and an adequate household staff. Strachan spent largely and in advance of his income, borrowing without compunction, importing furniture and prints, whatever his wife desired. Ann would have the complete home that she

presided over with such thoroughness. He would have that most useful of material blessings, a sufficient and unchanging base of opera-
tions. He expected to be in York some time.

To swell the family in the new house four more children were
eventually born – Alexander Wood, youngest of the boys, Agnes, and
two successive Emmas who each survived but a summer and died.

One further change had to be made if he was to be free to embark on
his projects, although it was long in coming. He had to rid himself of
the burden of teaching school every day. The Home District Grammar
School was never quite the consuming passion that Cornwall had been,
nor, said the boys who had been at both, was it ever quite as good. The
building was a raw two-storey structure, painted blue, the funds to
paint it raised by Strachan giving a series of public lectures in natural
philosophy. There were, of course, too many boys for one master. Instruction was given by a series of young men most of whom were also
studying for holy orders under Strachan's direction. It was an economi-
cal arrangement. They received bursaries of eighty pounds a year from
the Society for the Propagation of the Gospel and salaries of one hundred pounds a year as ushers. They read theology under Strachan, and
in some cases lived with him, taught school, and awaited the will of the
bishop who would ordain them. For their sake, and for that of his own
sons in school, Strachan held on to his schoolmastership longer than he
had intended. In the end, the adhesion to the church of a Scotch Presbyterian, Samuel Armour, presented him with a like-minded replacement.
At the age of forty-six Strachan brought to an end thirty years of teaching, with a feeling of relief that surprised even himself.

The parish of York continued to present him with an unbroken round of duties. Morning service on Sundays saw almost all the townspeople present. Evening service at three in the afternoon was more sparsely attended. Baptisms usually followed evening service as the Sunday schools preceded it. In between, prayers must be said at the jail and in the hospital. On one afternoon a month he went out to York Mills where a country congregation had been established. Sunday evenings remained clear of duty and were saved for the pleasures of family life. The labours of the parish spilled over into the other days of the week, of course, and the church fabric was for many years a care. St. James' Church on King Street had to be rebuilt, enlarged, and rebuilt again. But all of these were duties that Strachan had no desire to suspend or delegate to others. The schoolmaster had long since been lost in the parson, and however strangely Providence had brought him to this point, he knew himself to be in the noblest of the professions, and in the right church. Churchmanship can grow on one.

Churchmen assumed that the Church of England was the established church in Upper Canada, or rather, that the established church of the English nation was in Upper Canada and that this amounted to the same thing. No specific law of the Upper Canadian legislature had established the church (as an act of the first legislature of Nova Scotia had in that colony). No such law, they said, was necessary. The Constitutional Act of 1791, that British act which had created the two Canadas, had provided for the government of the church including the governor's right to make presentations to livings. In setting apart the clergy reserves it had made a future provision for the church in the form of an endowment in lands, a provision generous in the extreme, if largely prospective. Meanwhile the church was administered by governor and bishop in accordance with the body of British acts, orders in council, and despatches that had been accumulating since the conquest. The present needs of the church were being provided for out of revenue both British and colonial pending the rise in value of landed endowments.

No one believed that much had been accomplished by the church before the war's end. The human material had been too difficult. The French were obdurate in their Catholicism, the English the flotsam of a frontier, almost wholly unchurched, less than 5 per cent Church of England. Such emigrants as came in were more apt to be Americans than English, until at last the end of the wars brought hope again to the colony, and British settlers. Bishop Jacob Mountain and those who thought with him set themselves anew to extend the establishment.

The programme was straightforward. Every town and village should have its church, every township a sufficient number of clergymen. Every colonist was entitled to have that which he had left behind at home, access to the services of the church and to the ministrations of its clergy. He should not have to pay for those services. He did not do so at home. Collections there would always be, for charity was a good in itself, and Christians should participate in building churches and in sending the gospel to the heathen, but it was unwise to expect people to pay the salaries of their clergymen. The clergy would become dependents. Nor should such "voluntarism" be necessary once the munificent endowment of the reserves became productive. Until then other public sources and the private generosity of the English missionary societies, notably the Society for the Propagation of the Gospel, must be carefully used. Upper Canada deserved to have the best element in English civilization, the church.

All this was sweetly reasonable. If some dissenter objected that this set up a "dominant" church to the disadvantage of other churches it was clear that his premises were American rather than British. For all churches there would be complete toleration. No man suffered civil disabilities because of dissent. He could come to the highest appointed office, he could elect and be elected. The voluntary religious societies were given every freedom. It was charitable, but in the end unwise, to give them anything else. For in the English experience, voluntary societies flourished while their original zeal lasted, then died away. Most Englishmen could be expected to rise to, or lapse into, a decent conformity. An establishment provided for the continuing expression of the national religion, and the more knowledgeable dissenters accepted it as such.

Who would gainsay such a liberal and pious programme? The Roman Catholics could hardly do so. They had achieved a like status in Lower Canada and public support in the township of Glengarry where Catholic highlanders had been settled. The Church of Scotland supported the idea of an establishment, and as the legal establishment of part of the parent state asked for recognition. The convinced Protestant voluntarists, for whom the separation of church and state was a matter of belief, had what they wanted, separation. It was intolerant of them to wish to impose their belief on others. The Methodists, English and

American, had what they wanted, the religion of the frontier, a harvest of souls, circuit riders in the bush, a few cosy meeting-houses in the towns. The voluntary churches flourished in the destitute areas, ministering to those the church neglected. It was therefore the duty of the church to extend herself at once, or to run the risk of forfeiting forever the allegiance of the majority.

Such were the assumptions of the national church, shared by bishop and governor. John Strachan took over the whole set of ideas for his own. His detractors might think that this was a nimble bit of conformity in him. He had, after all, never seen England. No one could ever mistake him for an Englishman, and the sound of his voice as he read the prayer book offices always had an element of incongruity for those who first heard it. But then these were the assumptions of Scotland, with its identification of church and nation, its parochial system, and its parish schools, even more than of England. Indeed Strachan was always surprised at the incompleteness of the English in that they neglected the role of the church in common school education. The generality of the Scotch were members of their national church. It is true that that church had gone through reformations and disturbances that the English did not know, and that each new disturbance had left continuing pockets behind it, but the poverty of the land still made for conformity. Roman Catholicism survived in the west and the isles, Episcopalianism in Aberdeenshire, the covenanters in the southwest. Clan loyalties, isolation, ancient enmities, the "old cause" of Jacobitism, even theology, had kept the non-conforming elements alive. Disputes within the church itself continued to throw off new secessionist groups, Burghers and

Anti-Burghers, the Relief Church, and the followers of the brothers Haldane. Outsiders assumed it to be further evidence of Scotch faction. The parish churches, the schools, and the universities remained the province of the establishment. The Church of Scotland was secure, tolerant, dominated for forty years by men who called themselves "Moderatists" and eschewed Calvinism. Conformity was natural. Strachan's father had presumably been an Episcopalian, his mother a member of the Relief. Their son was being educated for the church. No mental somersaults were necessary. Dr. Strachan pursued the policies of his superiors with a whole heart, added his own "silent policy" that church and school must go hand in hand, and added, too, a cheerful Scotch contentiousness for the faith that surprised and sometimes alarmed the bishops.

Two small controversies engaged John Strachan in the immediate postwar period. Neither concerned the church nor his school and might well have been avoided.

Father Alexander Macdonell of Glengarry, "our friend the priest," sent Strachan a copy of the Earl of Selkirk's prospectus for the Red River settlement.[12] Settlement schemes of the Scotch by the Scotch were of interest to both men, and this one bristled with unnecessary difficulties. The prospectus had been addressed to potential proprietors and spoke of the profits to be made for absentee landlords by selling lands in the Red River Valley to assisted settlers. Selkirk might act from compassion, supported by dreams of empire. It was all too easy for John Strachan, using Sir Alexander Mackenzie's figures, to throw off a pamphlet exposing the inconsistencies. Merino sheep and hemp as possible

---

12 George Spragge, ed., *The Strachan Letter Book, 1812–1834* (Toronto: Ontario Historical Society, 1946), p. 83, Strachan to W. McGillivray, 2 May 1815.

Assiniboian staples were easily disposed of. If compassion was the motive, why not bring out emigrants to be landowners in Upper Canada rather than tenants at the end of the fearful walk from Hudson Bay? Indians, wild animals, and extremes of climate were cruel additional burdens for the noble lord's protégés to bear. That the Canadian fur trade should also be unfriendly was not to be wondered at. Strachan's part in the tangled business ended with his *Letter to the Earl of Selkirk*[13] and as the suits and countersuits dragged on he came to regret even that intervention. He was aware, at least briefly, that contentions might well be avoided by a man possessed of his accumulating offices.

A controversy with another Scotchman, Robert Gourlay, reversed Strachan's role. He maintained public silence while that gifted scribbler singled him out as the particular butt of his sarcasm. Dr. Strachan, Gourlay claimed, played amateur tricks with a philosophical apparatus and charged his captive audience a guinea a head to paint the school-house blue. Strachan, now so puffed up, had come out as a servant and tutor hired by one of Gourlay's wife's relations. (Mrs. Gourlay was a Hamilton.) Others of the lady's relations, and there were many, combined to send Gourlay back to her, but not before he had contrived to make himself a martyr and had driven the colonial authorities into a defensive conservatism. "A character like Mr. Gourlay in a quiet colony like this may do much harm,"[14] said Strachan afterwards. A pattern of criticism had been begun, and of criticism informed and worthy of respect, even though Gourlay's freakish humours tended to discredit it. In this instance the critic was silenced by repressive and archaic measures that Strachan protested against, but the criticism remained.

13   John Strachan, *Letter to the Right Honourable the Earl of Selkirk, on his settlement at the Red River, near Hudson's Bay* (London: Longman, Hurst, *et al.*, 1816).

14   Spragge, ed., *John Strachan Letter Book*, p. 185.

The first public agitation against the clergy reserves came in 1817 when a measure was introduced in the Assembly by Colonel Robert Nichol criticizing the reserves as obstacles to settlement, as "inducements to future wars," and as being "beyond all precedent lavish." Nichol asked only that the legislature make respectful representations to London to have a proportion of the lands sold at once and the proceeds used to build churches, but Strachan scented danger. Proposals soon came that the revenue be devoted to secular purposes. Once let the clergy lands become a matter of public debate and there would be no end. He wrote his bishop asking for new declarations of policy, by himself and by government. He urged an immediate and energetic policy of leasing. In 1819 he became chairman of the new Clergy Corporation for managing the clergy reserves.

Vacant lands dividing settlement were an obvious nuisance to those settlements. The difficulties need no pointing up. Every casual visitor to Upper Canada observed the patchwork of wasteland alternating with homestead, the more noticeable after traversing the continuous village of the Lower Canadian pattern of settlement. The most illiterate colonist was aware of the cost in isolation and human loneliness. He made no distinction between lands held by the crown for any purpose and land held by private speculators against a rise in value. It mattered little to him that the land speculators wanted the land to become productive as much as he did, that the crown wanted reliable lessees. Waste lands were a visible target for discontent. Clergy reserves were more vulnerable still. Given the assumptions of the establishment, the case for the clergy reserves was no different from that for any other endowment in the public interest held in trust for the nation. But a man must believe that the church and the nation were the same. If there were no clergy-man, no church, no services of the establishment, if such religious observances as his settlement knew were the product of his own will and that of his neighbours, if he had no reason to believe himself a member of the national church, then it was natural for him to believe that the reserves were the property of an alien religious denomination, a "would-be-dominant" church. No class of men was more liable to move the course of ideas in this direction than the itinerant Methodist clergy, especially those reared in the American concept of the separation of church and state. When, further, men came to believe that all crown reserves were in fact the possession of the electorate and subject to debate and disposal by the popular assembly, then the endowments were indeed in danger. John Strachan was fully aware of the possibilities. Given a fair trial, he believed that the establishment would gain majority support in the colony as at home. Yet he was realist enough not to hope for too much from the population as it then was. Too large a proportion were of American birth, too many had been reared without religion. The pattern of settlement had been hostile to the formation of neat parishes, dispersing men over the face of the whole province at once rather than in an orderly westward progression. Much more could be expected of the new British emigrants as they arrived. The most strenuous efforts must therefore be made that the national church might become not a devout idea but a presence in the land.

What strategy was possible? In the Assembly his own former pupils would do their duty. The Legislative Council he could look after himself, once he had asked for, and in 1820 received, appointment to it. The lieutenant governors were sound, Sir Peregrine Maitland, appointed in 1818, even more so than his predecessor. And behind them all stood the British parliament that had given the endowment when the lands lay empty above Kingston. No change, no alienation of the reserves from their sacred purposes, was possible without Parliament's consent. And as a direct consequence, public opinion in England had to be as sedulously cultivated in favour of the church as public opinion in the colony.

In 1819 Strachan began his assault upon the public of Upper Canada with that most potent weapon of propaganda, a newspaper. The religious press in America was thriving. Protestants of every breed fed upon weeklies and monthlies and in the absence of clergy formed their opinions upon those of distant editors. The church in the Canadas should have the like aid if Strachan could furnish it. For a year and a half he worked at it, amid all his other duties, and found that monthly journalism was a tangle of difficulties. The first volume of the *Christian Recorder* did not pay for itself. The second was also the last. Journals to be successful must possess the editor. Strachan would try again in later years when staff was available. Meanwhile he had tasted ink and tested local opinion.

It was Sir Peregrine Maitland and the business of the clergy reserves that first took Strachan to England in 1824. He had long wished for a holiday in Scotland, but the years passed without that possibility, and it was now a quarter-century since he had sailed from Greenock. His brother James had made one trip out to see him, had duly marvelled at the signs of success, and had been saddled with the authorship of John's little emigrant's guide.[15] He still sent money home to his sisters. But to go himself was impossible while school and church required attendance. In 1823 the schoolmastering had ended. He had accepted, instead, the presidency of the newly created Board for the General Superintendence of Education that gave him authority without daily duty. The parish could be left in the hands of a *locum tenens*. Government provided the necessary funds, for Sir Peregrine was anxious that the colony be represented by an informed agent, and off Strachan went by way of New York.

There was another reason to go in addition to the business of the reserves. Bishop Jacob Mountain's years were drawing to an end. The Honourable and Reverend Charles James Stewart, son of the Earl of Galloway and travelling missionary in the diocese of Quebec, was an obvious successor, and Strachan could not but welcome the prospect. Stewart had that form of saintliness he most admired, an evangelical piety that showed itself in a disciplined and self-denying life rather than in many words. Joined to it, he had acquired a knowledge of the two colonies second to none, gained by travel on horseback through all the settlements, and yet retained the most firm convictions as to the value of an establishment for the Canadas. But though Stewart was the logical next bishop, logic also suggested that there be two, and there were interesting and alarming possibilities. The appointments lay in the crown, as always, and it was the crown's advisers Strachan was going to see.

15   James Strachan, *A Visit to the Province of Upper Canada in 1819* (Aberdeen: D. Chalmers for James Strachan, 1820).

Archdeacon and Bishop

John Strachan came to England for the first time in the spring of 1824, in time for his forty-sixth birthday. He took up residence at 19, Bury Street in St. James and was at once involved with the Colonial Office. The most urgent business, and the most complex, concerned the clergy reserves. Behind all the physical and administrative problems, of leasing or of selling, of present value and likely increment, there lay the original question – for what purpose were they given? Strachan held to the simplest answer. They were an endowment for the Church of England, the gift of a pious king to the English national church. It was, of course, too simple. Whatever the ministry of 1791 had meant by "a Protestant clergy," and that was a matter of dispute, authority now resided in the current parliament, and Lord Bathurst in the Colonial Office needed solutions acceptable to government, to the law officers of the crown, to the English church, and, to a degree, to the population of Upper Canada. For Strachan there were other difficulties. However adamant a defender of the simple answer he might be in public, the bent of his mind was essentially practical. He might say that the principle of the single church establishment was everything. He would work for what would serve to strengthen that church in the parishes. He would also prefer to remain in the good graces of those in authority, in the process, and in the end, he would obey without question whatever became law.

In 1820 he had believed that the likeliest solution for the reserves was to appropriate a proportion of them for individual parishes, two to a township, thereby endowing the parishes at once and removing part of the reserves from public debate. What a parish owned would be inviolable. Maitland had demurred. Strachan now pressed upon Lord

Bathurst the policy of empowering the Clergy Corporation to sell up to half the reserves in any one area and to fund the money in Britain. The backwoodsman's objection to reserve lands lying derelict and separating him from his neighbour would disappear if the offending lots could in fact be sold. At this point the newly forming Canada Land Company confused the issue. They proposed to buy the crown reserves and one-half of the clergy reserves at once, at a price to be determined, an action which would have removed them as an object of contention for ever, if not the funds arising therefrom. An independent commission went out and returned with a recommended price of three shillings and sixpence an acre. Strachan, joined by Peter Robinson, chose to object. It was a calculated risk. Endless battles might have been avoided, but the land would bring in at least ten shillings an acre if sold with care, and there seemed no point in assenting to the waste of an ecclesiastical endowment for the sake of temporary peace. After three years of negotiation, the Canada Company was given the Huron Tract and other crown lands as an alternative, but meanwhile a solution to the clergy reserves was postponed.

In May came more business for the Colonial Office. Government proposed a union of the two Canadian legislatures and to Andrew Stuart, member of the Legislative Assembly for Quebec, was given the task of preparing a suitable bill. Would Dr. Strachan join with his former pupil in the work of revision and give his opinions? Strachan fell to work with many misgivings. He found difficulty working with Andrew. Few men in the upper province favoured union with the turbulent French Canadians. Most of all, a union would be of disadvantage to the church, for the hoped-for majority position in Upper Canada would be lost forever. The Roman Catholic vote under any modification of the franchise or of representation, if joined to that of dissent, would swamp the church interest. He produced, as he was asked, a reasoned analysis of the bill, and of the revisions he preferred. They were essentially the solutions judged necessary by Poulett Thomson in the Union of 1841: the containment of the French voting force, the introduction of municipal institutions in Lower Canada, the location of the capital in Upper Canada, and an imperial settlement of the clergy reserves. None of it was more than the best of a bad job.[1]

Then, although he was not asked, he produced a union plan of his own as an alternative. The objects looked for in uniting the Canadas might be better achieved by uniting all of the provinces, the Canadas and the maritimes. In concert with John Robinson he produced for the benefit of the Colonial Office *Observations on the policy of a General Union of all the British Provinces of North America*.[2] It was a federal union he contemplated, the members of the general legislature elected by and from the legislative assemblies or appointed from their councils. Most powers would remain in the provinces, but the French would be contained and conceivably anglicized, and the united provinces could grow to nationhood under the crown. It remained a sketch only, finished off by May the twenty-fourth. Strachan had no knowledge of the maritimes, no great trust in the Montreal English, no animus against the French. He might speak of Halifax and St. John and St. Andrews as becoming ocean ports for the Canadas, but there was no suggestion as to how the intervening distances were to be overcome. His point of

1 [John Strachan], *Observations on a Bill for uniting the Legislative Councils and Assemblies of the Provinces of Lower and Upper Canada in one Legislature* ... (London: W. Clowes, 1824).
2 London: W. Clowes, 1824.

view was York, his interest the church, and he could be as narrowly provincial as the next man. But meanwhile it was exhilarating work being an empire-builder and dreaming up constitutions for an appreciative Bathurst.

Finally there was the business of the succession. Bathurst apparently agreed that the aged Bishop Mountain should be succeeded by two bishops, one for each colony. The difficulty was financial. Mountain's salary of three thousand pounds came from Britain. A second British salary was impossible. The church funds in the colony were not yet productive. Charles James Stewart, in London on diocesan business, knew himself destined to be bishop of Quebec. He was somewhat wryly aware that Strachan was eager to undertake Upper Canada. Meanwhile the matter must rest upon events. The two men were to take ship together from Liverpool to New York in October, Strachan in the belief that Bathurst would give him the bishopric, or as an interim measure, make him archdeacon.

Late in July, as soon as circumstances permitted, he toured Scotland. He spent a Sunday in the manse at Kettle as an honoured guest, then rode on to St. Andrews to stay with Thomas Duncan, now a professor in the university. They called on Thomas Chalmers, professor of moral philosophy, and recalled old times. It was a sweet triumph to be home among friends yet demonstrably successful in the old Scotch game of getting on in the Englishman's world. "Getting on" was a duty one owed one's friends and one's family. He visited Aberdeen and his mother's grave in St. Nicholas' churchyard, made a quick visit to Edinburgh to see Dr. Brown, and then took ship again for London preparatory to going home. It had been an entirely successful trip. "The English," he used to say afterwards, "are cool to you at first, but persevere and they give you their friendship." Lord Bathurst and the undersecretary, Wilmot Horton, had been persevered with, and were kindness itself.

He came home to York in November to find a new grave in the family plot. A fourth daughter Emma had been born and had died, without having been seen by her father. Life resumed in the midst of some sadness. Then in June of 1825 the long-declining Jacob Mountain died. Strachan lost no time. On the Sunday following the reception of the news he preached a memorial sermon to his congregation in St. James' Church. Subsequently printed, it was and remained a full statement of the assumptions of the establishment. Scotland and England owed all that they were under God to their national churches. Upper Canada had a right to share in the benefits of the parent state. Much had been granted in the Constitutional Act. Much had been effected by the late bishop of Quebec. More was to be expected if Britain would support the church as she should. There were difficulties, and in stating them Strachan was to enlarge them. "Uneducated itinerant preachers ... leaving their steady employment, betake themselves to preaching the gospel from idleness, or a zeal without knowledge, by which they are induced without any preparation to teach what they do not know, and which from their pride they disdain to learn." Again, "the religious teachers of the other denominations of Christians, a very few respectable Ministers of the Church of Scotland excepted, come almost universally from the Republican States of America."[3] Such a challenge would not pass unanswered, but on that July morning Strachan felt confident for his church.

3 John Strachan, *A Sermon, preached at York, Upper Canada, third of July, 1825, On the Death of the late Lord Bishop of Quebec* (Kingston: Macfarlane, 1826).

Stewart went home that month to be consecrated second bishop of Quebec. There was still to be only one bishop, but Bathurst informed Stewart in August that to be of some aid in diocesan administration he was creating the archdeaconry of York and appointing Dr. Strachan thereto, at an additional salary of three hundred pounds a year.

Meanwhile there was progress in the matter of the reserves. After continued alarms, the Canada Company had settled for other crown lands instead of those set apart for the clergy. Moreover, out of the purchase money paid in by the company the lieutenant governor was ordered to set apart funds of seven hundred and fifty pounds a year for the benefit of the Church of Scotland and the Roman Catholic clergy. The way was now open to return to the earlier scheme of selling part of the reserves. But even as these developments were going forward Strachan was sent once more to England, and on business more delightful still.

The agreeable Maitland had been induced by his advisers late in 1825 to ask for an exchange of salable crown lands, in lieu of the blocks of wild land long set apart for higher education, so that a university for the colony might no longer be delayed. Archdeacon Strachan was the obvious person to further the project, so again he made the March journey overland to New York and again took up residence in Bury Street in April 1826.

The complexities of the business kept him there seventeen months. Not till March 1827 would Bathurst's despatch be completed: "His Majesty has been pleased to grant a Royal Charter by Letters Patent under the great Seal for establishing at or near the Town of York in the Province of Upper Canada one College, with the Style and privileges of an University ... to continue for ever, to be called King's College." An exchange of crown reserves would provide an immediate endowment. A thousand pounds a year was available from Canada Company payments to erect buildings. Construction could begin almost at once and instruction not long after.

The terms of the charter involved some compromise between what Strachan thought useful and what he could get. British universities were connected with the established church, whether Scotch or English. There was no doubt that King's College, York, must be. The visitor would be the bishop of Quebec, the chancellor the lieutenant governor, the president the Archdeacon of York. The professors and all members of the college council would subscribe to the Thirty-Nine Articles. Only the students were free to belong to any church or to none, and students in divinity must still be churchmen. Never before, said Strachan, had the crown granted so liberal a charter. It was, of course, not liberal enough for Upper Canada. Limiting membership on the council to Church of England men eliminated some potentially useful persons. Having only English clergy as professors (for professors were inevitably clergymen) would prevent the recruiting of like-minded persons from the Scotch universities. And the identification of the presidency with the archdeaconry of York was an embarrassment. Strachan intended, of course, to bring the university to birth, but not to remain forever archdeacon. His successor might not be an academic. The interests of the church would have been effectively secured by the requirement that visitor and president be churchmen, and fewer dissenters offended. Clearly Bathurst, or James Stephen, his permanent counsel, subscribed to the idea of the English establishment even more consistently than did Strachan himself. Strachan was content. He knew this to be the great triumph of his life, and promptly began to create the myth that it was for this cause that he had first come to Canada in 1799.

The university required other services of him while the opportunity offered. He called upon the great church societies to bespeak grants for books. The Society for the Propagation of the Gospel and the Society for Promoting Christian Knowledge both complied to the amount of five hundred pounds. The Church Missionary Society, with fine imagination, offered a hundred pounds a year for a professor of Indian languages, and the same sum for scholarships to train young men as Indian missionaries. And again for books and for information he went down to Oxford and to Cambridge and was caught up in the riot and ceremony of an Oxford commemoration.

In October of 1826 he had his holiday, taking the sea voyage to Scotland, visiting Aberdeen, Edinburgh, and St. Andrews. In the chapel of St. Andrews he preached before Chalmers and Duncan and the rest of the faculty, apostate from Presbyterianism though he was. Two years later his friends secured for him the honorary degree of doctor of laws of that university.

The Scottish holiday was cut short by a summons from the Colonial Office. Wilmot Horton, chairman of a parliamentary select committee on emigration, wanted Strachan's opinions upon the committee's report. It was the kind of exercise he could not resist, and he threw himself into it. England and parts of Scotland had redundant populations. The parishes were spending large sums annually to maintain life in the poor, and the poor, given subsidies but not hope, degenerated. The English parish rates must continue to increase and to provide no remedy. Instead, let parliament now provide sums sufficient to remove to British North America all the poor who were willing to go and to support them there for the first twelve to eighteen months. The initial costs would be considerable, and he gives the figures. The ultimate saving would warrant it, and he gives more. But the savings in persons would be the principal good, of families able to stand on their own feet on their own land, self-respecting and restored to hope. No people did better in Upper Canada than the laborious poor and he gives figures on settlement and case histories of success.[4] They threshed out the subject together in London and for three days in a Brighton hotel. Wilmot Horton had him to dine with T. R. Malthus and Thomas Tooke, the economists, and with John Gibson Lockhart of the *Quarterly Review*, but government-assisted emigration on any large scale was an unlikely proposition in that spring of political upheaval.

Lord Bathurst left the Colonial Office in April 1827 with the break-up of Liverpool's ministry, and an era was over. Strachan could rejoice that his university was safely through. There remained the act to sell a part of the clergy reserves. A simple bill had been introduced into parliament in February before the old ministry had been dissolved. Edward George Stanley, heir to the Earl of Derby and fresh from a tour of Canada, asked the unwelcome question: who were the "Protestant clergy" mentioned in the Canada Act? Second reading was postponed

---

4   John Strachan, *Remarks on emigration from the United Kingdom ... addressed to Robert Wilmot Horton ...* (London: John Murray, 1827).

while further information could be procured. Strachan spent some hurried days supplying it, and from such material as he had at hand produced a forty-page pamphlet, *Observations on the provision made for the maintenance of a Protestant Clergy in the provinces of Upper and Lower Canada*, together with an "Ecclesiastical Chart of the Province of Upper Canada."[5] The "Protestant clergy" in the plain meaning of the Act were of the Church of England alone. In Upper Canada successively wider interpretations had been attempted, in favour of an equal establishment of the Scotch church and in favour of all protestant sects. The latest proposal had been to divert the funds to the support of education. With clarity and some vehemence Strachan denounced all such alternatives. He need not have worried. The Colonial Office had no intention of bringing the Church of Scotland to an equal position with the Church of England in Upper Canada. It would have set a precedent for India and Jamaica and all the rest, and no government could contemplate the charges likely from two establishments. The bill became law in July. John Robinson's brother Peter, commissioner of crown lands, began selling the reserves in 1829 and at an average price of over fourteen shillings an acre. There were safeguards. Only one hundred thousand acres could be sold in one year. Three to four hundred acres were to be saved in each township for a glebe. At last the lands were on their way to becoming a funded endowment at a reasonable price.

Archdeacon Strachan sailed from Portsmouth, England, on July 5, 1827, and came home believing that he had achieved much for church and state. The triumph was short-lived. York was agitated by a fury of protest, much of it directed against himself.

5   John Strachan, *Observations on the provision made for the maintenance of a Protestant Clergy in the provinces of Upper and Lower Canada* ... (London: R. Gilbert, 1827).

Early in his absence, a wild journalist and Dundonian, William Lyon Mackenzie, had been saved from bankruptcy by the irresponsible action of a group of young men who threw his type into the bay. Mackenzie, given damages by the court, now baited the administration with renewed vigour and the consciousness of rectitude. Of far more importance, the Methodists had found a champion in a twenty-four-year-old preacher, Egerton Ryerson, who attacked first the sermon on the death of Mountain and then the *Observations* in a series of widely reprinted letters. Strachan was embarrassed to discover that he had erred, in propriety, in facts, and in tactics. The impropriety was there in a sentence of the Ecclesiastical Chart: "One of the two remaining clergymen in communion with the Church of Scotland has applied to be admitted into the Established Church."[6] That had been privileged information and could only result in injured denials. The accuracy of the facts was a relative matter. "As the Methodists have no settled clergymen," he had written, "it has been found difficult to ascertain the number of itinerants employed, but it is presumed to be considerable, perhaps from twenty to thirty in the whole province; one from England settled at Kingston appears to be a very superior person." In fact, there were forty in 1827, forty-six after the next meeting of Conference. Of these only eight or nine were Americans. Such errors in mathematics were damaging, but could be borne, as could Ryerson's personal abuse of "the little Rector" and "Hamaan." "Whenever he is animated in pleading for preferment, power or money, which is generally no oftener than he has an opportunity"[7] was shrewdly put, when his labours had produced salaries of three hundred pounds for the archdeaconry and two

6 *Ibid.*, "Ecclesiastical Chart," facing p. 24.
7 York, *Colonial Advocate*, 11 Nov. 1827.

hundred and fifty for the presidency, but they were monies earned. Ryerson incidentally denied the doctrine of the apostolic succession as Episcopalians understood it, but doctrines could stand for themselves, secure against the judgment of the world.

What was truly damaging were not the personalities or the statistics, but the fact that the idea of an establishment was now under an eager and sustained criticism. Ryerson spoke of the church as "the fewest in number of any five or six denominations," of the university as based on "sectarian principles," and the debate in the Assembly and the press echoed such phrases. A church can only be called national as long as the general will of the population consents to it. Call it a sect or one more denomination and the idea is destroyed. The old assumptions of the establishment were now challenged, in the very hour when they were taking practical shape, and could never again be taken for granted.

Strachan knew that he had offended and kept public silence until the storm should abate, save for one elaborate *apologia* delivered in the Legislative Council in March.[8] As if to mark the passing of an old order, Sir Peregrine Maitland was removed to the more governable colony of Nova Scotia by an anxious Colonial Office. Churchmen cannot be changed so conveniently, but the new governor, Sir John Colborne, believed that Strachan's political involvement had been damaging to the church and plainly regarded him as minister of his parish church but not his chief political adviser.

The parish of York went its usual way, and its minister was kept busy with the services in St. James', now grown too small, with three or four points outside, with the weddings, baptisms, and funerals of a

---

8   John Strachan, *A speech, of the Venerable John Strachan, D.D. archdeacon of York, in the Legislative council, Thursday, sixth March, 1828: on the subject of the clergy reserves* (York: Stanton, 1828).

rapidly rising population. There were still young men training for orders and sometimes a curate to assist him, and even occasionally Bishop Stewart who chose to live sometimes in this more thriving end of his diocese.

The office of archdeacon had brought new duties. Strachan was responsible for the clergy and the missions in the western two-thirds of the province, and in August of 1828 he set out to visit each of them for himself. By waggon and horse he made his first thorough excursion into the hinterland, through the Niagara peninsula, west along the Governor's Road to Sandwich, and back again. Driving from Chatham south and east towards Talbot Street and the Lake Erie front in response to a request for a service, he and his party became mired in the bush road. They left the waggon and pressed on in the growing dark until they were thoroughly lost. He spent the night protected from the rain and storm by a tree trunk, wet through, but enjoying the company of his own thoughts. In the dawn they found a settler's cabin and went on to the road and to an inn and a hastily summoned church service.[9] At fifty, he rejoiced to find that his rude health held, and that this long-empty country was beginning to fill with English and Irish emigrants who might welcome the Episcopalian services that the older settlers had done so long without. "It is not what we are," he would declare afterwards, "but what we may become."

In October he made a similar journey eastward. Admittedly the eastern districts were Archdeacon Stuart's responsibility, but Strachan's office as president of the Board for the General Superintendence of Education gave reason enough that he should visit the grammar schools

9   Ernest Hawkins, *Annals of the diocese of Toronto* (London: S.P.C.K., 1848), p. 115.

and consult in each district town the records of the government-assisted common schools. The pattern was the same. He inspected the works of the Rideau canal going forward under Colonel By, preached and baptized as required by day, dined at night, and moved on through the settlements scanning the land.

Strachan's scheme for education involved a centralized system of common schools in each township and grammar schools in each district, managed locally, but controlled by an annual legislative grant administered by a general board that answered only to the governor. The board parcelled out the additional funds, approved textbooks, and presumably provided unity and oversight. Strachan attempted to ensure that all the grammar school masters, and some at least of the common school teachers, be clergymen of one of the national churches. He tried, at one time, to persuade Bishop Mountain to license the lay teachers as catechists, with authority to read the service and to preach on Sundays. In Scotland schoolmasters subscribed to the confession of faith. In England grammar school masters were licensed by the ordinary. In Upper Canada school trustees hired whom they could, while Strachan worked towards uniformity and the church connection. Ideally education would be free at the primary and secondary levels and Strachan had long since recommended that crown reserves be set aside to endow them. Until the school lands became productive, the common schools would need to charge fees of four or five dollars a scholar in addition to what assistance the general board could give. Poor young men should be given scholarships of ten pounds a year to enable them to attend grammar school. Instruction at the district schools would include French, Latin, arithmetic, geography, and practical mathematics, thus reflecting Strachan's old preference for combining the academic and the useful. Regrettably the legislature, hard pressed for funds and jealous of its by-passed authority, cut the appropriations, and common school education faltered.[10]

Meanwhile, there was the university to plan for. President Strachan found the site he wanted, a hundred and fifty acres to the northwest of the town, pleasant rising land with a creek, the Taddle, running through it, and two hundred acres of glebe land available to the north. He persuaded the owners of the park lots concerned to sell, at twenty-five pounds an acre, and at once laid out access roads to Yonge Street and Lot (later Queen) Street. The next step would be buildings and professors. Strachan knew what he wanted: a college for the liberal arts and sciences where boys coming up from the grammar schools could combine humane and useful studies, and then go out to take their part in the life of the colony. Teaching could hardly begin for another two or three years until the lands had been exchanged and sold and an income secured, but in the interim there were fences to build and rows of chestnut trees to plant, and Strachan found himself regularly drawn to walk the three quarter-mile stretch from his house.

Suddenly, in December 1828, there was a set-back. Sir John Colborne, the newly arrived governor, exercised his office as chancellor by summoning the college council and informing them that building must be postponed until he had the opportunity of submitting the charter to the legislature for possible revision.

Sir John's action appeared to be a politic gesture in favour of democracy. It soon developed that he had educational ideas of his own, gained

10 Judson Douglas Purdy, "John Strachan and Education in Canada, 1800–1851," Ph.D. thesis, University of Toronto, 1962.

from three years' governing in the Channel Islands. He now proceeded to commit the university funds to building and staffing what he considered a prior requirement, an English classical preparatory school. Upper Canada College came into existence in consequence, absorbing the staff and students, and for a while the building, of the Home District Grammar School. Half a dozen first-class masters were imported who entered upon a proper English curriculum, solidly classical and mathematical. Strachan again could hardly disagree in public. It was not for him to fight against the Latin. His youngest son, Alexander, must be a pupil. He observed sardonically, as Baldwin, Ryerson, and others raised their objections, that this was hardly catering to the democracy, or to the education that he thought desirable. There was one incidental benefit. The governor's masters turned out, somewhat inevitably, to be Church of England clergymen, and Strachan had the pleasure of seeing them in the pews of St. James', or of using them to take services in the country.

St. James' Church had to be rebuilt, even if the university must wait. Again Strachan found himself at cross-purposes with his governor. The rector and wardens petitioned for a grant of a thousand pounds towards rebuilding. Sir John sent on the petition with a counterproposal of his own, that government build a church in the west end for the troops. The Colonial Office chose to assist the parish church rather than to build another, and the new St. James' rose on the old site, magnificent, seemly, seating three thousand persons, rich with walnut, the pews furnished to their owners' tastes. Pew number one, lined with crimson, housed the minister's family.

The Strachan family was now beginning to contract. The house facing the bay had been filled for years with growing children, assorted relations, and friends, with theological students and the domestic staff. The expense was considerable, but Strachan valued the method of his wife and the ordered riot of his household. The first to leave was James McGill Strachan. He had grown up hobnobbing with the officers of the garrison next door and desired above all things to be one himself. Strachan bought him his commission for fifteen hundred pounds and sent the boy off to a life in Europe he both deplored and took pride in. "Captain James" was always the prized first fruits of his own success in life, knowledgeable, accepted, and assured.

Elizabeth's health gave some cause for anxiety, and when she was seventeen Strachan decided that she must have sea air and a sight of the world, so in the summer of 1831 he took her on an extended holiday at the heart of which were eight days in Halifax as the guests of Sir Peregrine Maitland and Lady Sarah. The sea voyages required prostrated him as much as his daughter, from Boston to Halifax, across the Bay of Fundy to St. John, and five days in a gale from the New Brunswick border to Portland, but a young lady rising eighteen is matter of much astonishment and delight to a male parent, and moreover Elizabeth's health improved.[11] A year later she was married in St. James' to a young man of good family and even better income, Thomas Mercer Jones, commissioner of the Canada Company. The Strachans had the pleasure of helping to superintend the building of a most elegant villa for them on a parcel of the family lot.[12] Elizabeth was to remain a member of the family circle until the interests of the Canada Company took the Joneses to live in Goderich in the thirties.

11 Alexander Neil Bethune, *Memoir of the Right Reverend John Strachan, First Bishop of Toronto* (Toronto: Henry Rowsell, 1870), p. 153.
12 John Howard's plans for the Jones villa are given in Marion MacRae and Anthony Adamson, *The Ancestral Roof* (Toronto: Clarke, Irwin, 1963).

Son George left York for Kingston to train for the law, for George, somehow, was always better off away from home. John appeared to be the cleverest but the hardest to provide for. In his father's judgment he was "simple and artless in his manners and disposition, and will require as the old Scotch schoolmaster used to say, some of the Devil in in order to keep the Devil out."[13] He studied for the law in York with some inclination for commerce. The handsome Alexander, day boy at Upper Canada, and sharp little Agnes, now turned ten, provided at home the company of children's minds that the long-time dominie in Strachan always required. Years afterwards, he was to recollect with pleasure that "we delighted in the children when young."[14]

Emigrants were now pouring into the province from the British Isles. Fifteen to twenty thousand came upriver each year and most of them descended upon York on their way west. In the summer of 1832 and again in 1834, the asiatic cholera came up with them, inexorably making its way from Quebec to Montreal to the wharves at the foot of Yonge Street. Its symptoms were diarrhoea, vomiting, cramps, and merciful insensibility; its normal outcome death within twenty-four hours. In the summer of 1832 its results by Strachan's figures were four hundred deaths, nearly four hundred fatherless children, about ninety new widows.[15]

The epidemic provided exactly the kind of crisis that John Strachan was most fitted for, and York was to remember the time of the cholera as his most meritorious hour. He had boundless energy and health. He was not unduly sensitive. He had no fear of death. He could stand the filth and vomit and foul air without a qualm. If in God's providence

13 Strachan Papers, Strachan to Mrs. Brown, 28 Sept. 1833.
14 *Ibid.*, Strachan to Ann Strachan, 22 July 1851.
15 PAO, Strachan Letter Book, 1827–34 (SLB 1827–34), Strachan to Richard Whatley, archbishop of Dublin, 24 Sept. 1832.

he died, then he died. As others went off he said prayers, looked after the survivors, arranged the burials, and went on. His curate fell ill at the first sight of the cholera wards. Strachan recognized the diversities of gifts, forbade him further sick duty, and did it alone. The record of one climactic week-end, in August of 1834, tells the story. He was home on Saturday night by nine, resting from the day, when the call came to go out again. He returned at 5 A.M., to find his waggon ready to take him to an interment in the country at six. He was home again by eight and off at once for a service at the garrison, the troops not being permitted to come into town. He did the garrison hospital afterwards, crossed town to bury nine persons in the churchyard, and was just in time for morning service at eleven. Before the afternoon service at three he had said prayers in the jail and the general hospital. After service, he made sick calls, dined, buried eight more persons, and returned to the hospital.

The epidemic would cease in September, but the wreckage of families remained: orphans, widows with fatherless broods, most of them emigrants, destitute and bewildered, their small plans gone. The task was to find them homes and subsistence. In 1832 Strachan formed a society for their relief, collected funds, appealed most of all for the farmers and others to come in from the surrounding townships and take these people into their homes. There was one pitiful concomitant. The families broken by cholera must in many cases be broken further. Brothers and sisters would be separated. Mothers must be persuaded, urged, bullied into parting with their children. You did what you could. The farmers of Trafalgar Township came in in a body and took back widows and children together. They made a useful example to cite. There was no guarantee that other children were not being given up bound to the care of some rural tyrant. "And in this manner," in the words of Strachan's appeal, "much of the bitterness of this sad dispensation would be removed by Christian love."[16]

The time of the cholera coincided with a period of truce in the religious and political struggles of Upper Canada, and Strachan found himself both appreciated and somewhat mellowed. The citizens of York presented him with a silver table ornament worth a hundred guineas. His old boys at Cornwall banded together and gave him an epergne of silver and crystal engraved with their names and with their current offices. He confessed to a friend in Scotland that his life's work might be largely over and that he might have to be content with what had been accomplished. The university must wait for another to begin. The diocese moved forward steadily under other hands than his, with new monies raised by new societies, new missions opened under new men. Bishop Charles James Stewart lived in York in the winter months and dealt with government and the missions with his usual discreet and unremitting care. The town of York grew and changed and became the city of Toronto in 1834, and William Lyon Mackenzie as its first mayor showed the incompetence one could expect of a radical in office. Strachan's own official duties decreased. The Legislative Assembly had contrived that the Board for the General Superintendence of Education be abolished in 1833; in 1835 he resigned as a member of the Executive Council on a "hint" from the Colonial Office. The years of his political influence seemed to be over, although he still attended occasionally upon the Legislative Council, angrily rebutting a second suggestion that he resign from that.

16   "Appeal of the Society for the Relief of the Orphan, Widow and Fatherless," York, *Christian Guardian*, 30 Jan. 1833, as quoted in Edith Firth, ed., *The Town of*

Bishop Stewart called a visitation in York, a meeting of all the clergy of Upper Canada, in September 1832. Strachan, in the midst of all the arrangement for the wrack of the cholera, preached the sermon, and used the occasion to speak well of the Presbyterians and of the Methodists. The latter were going through a doubly taming experience. The British and American streams, respectable Wesleyan emigrants and native "saddlebags," were about to come together in a short and uneasy union, and government was providing state funds for them (although not out of the clergy reserves). "Henceforth," said Strachan, "it is expected that the piety and zeal of [Wesley's] followers in this Colony will be directed by his spirit, and that having assumed his mantle and unfurled his banner, they will cherish the same friendly disposition towards our Establishment which their brethren do in England."[17]

The relative calm was broken by two persons. Sir John Colborne, on the brink of recall, created the crown rectories in January of 1836. Charles James Stewart had a seizure in his home in York in April and never wholly recovered his health.

The creation of the rectories was a straightforward action by a governor anxious to do his full duty. The Constitutional Act of 1791 had made provision for the division of the colony into parishes and for the institution of incumbents. Bathurst had directed Sir Peregrine Maitland to put the relevant portions of the act into effect, but difficulties had intervened. Lord Goderich in the Colonial Office had sent a characteristically ambiguous despatch in 1831. Colborne was simply tidying up unfinished business. Fifty-seven patents were made out constituting the rectories (although thirteen were never completed). An average of

York, 1815–1834 (Toronto: Champlain Society, 1966), p. 255.
17   John Strachan, Church fellowship. A sermon ... (York: Stanton, 1832).

four hundred acres from that part of the reserves kept from sale in each township and from other crown lands was assigned and deeded over to each parish as an individual endowment. For each rectory so constituted and endowed another document was made out presenting the incumbent named to the bishop to be instituted and inducted into the living. Strachan approved, although the initiative was Colborne's and the details the work of John Beverley Robinson. The established church was at last taking its usual local form: crown parishes, endowed at least partially with crown lands, served by a crown-appointed rector. Those who did not believe in an establishment were aroused into an instant and sustained protest.

Sir John Colborne left York on a winter's day in a train of sleighs, seen off by the whole populace paying tribute to his soldierly virtues. His replacement, Sir Francis Bond Head, came in knowing that the colony was in a turmoil over grievances, of which the new question of the rectories was the most clamant.

The illness of Bishop Stewart revived the hope of the episcopal succession. He was only sixty, Strachan's senior by three years less a day, but his self-denying labours and bachelor existence had taken their toll. There was no doubt what Stewart wanted to happen. The diocese of Quebec should be divided by government and he would take Upper Canada. The obvious candidate for Lower Canada would be the archdeacon of Quebec, the gentle and scholarly George Mountain, son to Jacob. As an alternative measure, Mountain should become a suffragan or assistant bishop with the right of succession to the whole. Stewart was strongly seconded by Sir John Colborne, who, through his aide-de-camp, informed the reluctant Mountain that it was his duty to accept consecration if only to eliminate his "competitor."[18] In the end the dutiful Mountain went to England to conduct the negotiations in person, and was consecrated by the archbishop in February 1836.

John Strachan was distressed. He could take no exception to Stewart. The man was sound, an evangelical without weakness or wordiness. He had fought hard for the establishment against successive ministers, even though, in Strachan's eyes, he lacked political sense or any liking for the game. He had, moreover, spent his life in the provinces and had covered them repeatedly from end to end. Nor could he object to George Mountain, either to the man or to his proceedings. Mountain plainly showed that he had no desire to rule the church in Upper Canada and asked for a division into two dioceses. When Stewart went home to die, Mountain succeeded to the title but continued to call himself "bishop of Montreal" as a reminder to all that one single diocese for the Canadas was an impossibility.

Strachan wanted to be bishop in Toronto. There was the old need to succeed. "It would be deeply mortifying to me," he wrote, "to be superseded by a stranger; for the best men like to rise in their own profession, and he that is disappointed at my age can scarcely console himself with the hope of future promotion."[19] But John Strachan was no longer seeking appointments for their own sake, as part of the process of getting on. He would not be the first careerist, or the last, who was caught and changed by the duties and opinions that can lie in ambush behind office. For the next three years until he was successful he used every occasion to press his claims. Successive lieutenant governors, Head and Sir

18 Thomas Reagh Millman, *The Life of the Right Reverend, the Honourable Charles James Stewart* (London: Huron College, 1953), p. 151.
19 Public Archives of Canada (PAC), Q, vol. 410, part 2, p. 428, Strachan to Sir George Arthur, 14 May 1838.

George Arthur, officially recommended him. His old ally Alexander Macdonell, Bishop of Regiopolis, wrote in his favour. The clergy of Upper Canada met in convention and recommended division of the diocese. He applied directly to the Colonial Office until the godly and dilatory Charles Grant, Lord Glenelg, replied, "It is with extreme concern that I find the arrangements ... have been productive of the disappointment so strongly expressed by the Archdeacon."[20] There were two facts against him. The Church of England had never yet appointed to one of her sees anyone other than an English gentleman, which Strachan demonstrably was not. Secondly he was too closely identified in the colonial mind with an outgoing social and political order. Sir George Arthur spoke to the first when he privately advised against appointing a Scotchman. Sir John Colborne had spoken for the other. Bishops must be impartial and above politics (unless, that is, they had a vote in the House of Lords).

Strachan had an avowed personal interest in crowning his career with a mitre, but behind the ambition lay something else, an awareness of the possibility of a new kind of episcopate in the colonial church. In 1832 he had written up the life of a man he much admired, the late John Henry Hobart, bishop of New York.[21] It was probably the best pamphlet he ever wrote, a product of the quiet months before the cholera. There were elements of self-advertisement in it, as always. Hobart was a good man to have known. Its form, "A letter" to the Reverend Thomas Chalmers, identified him with an older friend still, a man revered in Britain as preacher, professor, and worker in the Glasgow slums. But essentially the book was an examination of a new development in the *ecclesia*

20   PAC, G 1, vol. 77, p. 291, Glenelg to Head, 30 June 1856, no. 69.
21   John Strachan, *A Letter to the Rev. Thomas Chalmers, D.D. ... on the life and character of the Right Reverend Dr. Hobart, Bishop of New-York, North-America* (New York: Swords, Stanford, 1832).

Anglicana, Episcopalianism proclaimed as the true church yet operating successfully as an aggressive American denomination. Hobart had been the complete orthodox churchman, convinced that there could be no co-operation with those outside. He had propagated the faith by every means at his disposal – tracts, societies, seminaries, periodicals. He had deliberately sought controversy. He had extended the church's ministry throughout the state of New York, planting missions in all the new towns from the Hudson Valley to Lake Erie. And he had done all this within the framework of an American denomination with its democratically elected diocesan and general conventions. On one point only was Hobart wrong, in Strachan's view. He had toured England and had come to the conclusion that the establishment was a hindrance, that the church needed the freedom to be herself in a secular society. For seven pages Strachan wrote of his own arguments to persuade Hobart otherwise, that church and nation must be one. Hobart had not been convinced.

There remained three basic conclusions to be drawn from Hobart's life. The highest doctrine of the church as being of the will of Christ, and Episcopalianism, reformed yet apostolic, as the true present-day manifestation of it, if faithfully preached, laid hold upon men's loyalty. The organization of the church into joint conventions of bishops, priests, and laity utilized men's service and, under God, procured the election of worthy bishops. And thirdly, an apostolic man of the mind of Hobart, bold, wise, and diligent, could make a notable contribution.

By the spring of 1838 it was evident that the Colonial Office would agree to divide the diocese, but they were not prepared to provide an additional salary. Strachan proposed that he be appointed on his existing emoluments as archdeacon and rector until the reserves should become sufficiently productive. Glenelg replied in January 1839, "I have now to direct you to signify to the parties concerned that Her Majesty's Government, after consulting with the Archbishop of Canterbury, acquiesce in the Archdeacon's proposal."[22] John Strachan and Upper Canada had a bishopric.

The events of the years between Stewart's death and his own consecration were somewhat anticlimactic for Strachan. They saw a tory reaction and a radical rebellion, the "spirited" régime of Francis Bond Head and the irresponsible treason of Mackenzie. For John Strachan there was little that was unexpected. British emigrants had been pouring into the country; it was natural that British moderation should prevail. Mackenzie's mad escapade revealed him for what he was; his defeat without the aid of regular troops by the people of Upper Canada bespoke the soundness of the colony. Sir Francis, for some reason, held his council of war in Strachan's study on the night before the affair at Montgomery's Tavern, so that the Archdeacon had the opportunity of helping to shelve MacNab's plan of a pre-dawn attack and of planning the successful noonday march of the militia up Yonge Street. His son, Captain James, served as aide-de-camp to Colonel FitzGibbon. But there was no glory for anyone in that sorry business of murder and houseburning and funerals to follow. A month before, Strachan's own second son, George Cartwright, had died, unmarried, unsuccessful, his life all but unrecorded.

One important matter went forward, the university. There had never

22   PAC, G 1, vol. 91, p. 47, Glenelg to Arthur, 2 Jan. 1839, no. 192.

been any dearth of solutions to that problem. Each session of the Assembly produced some. Bishop Stewart had suggested dividing the endowment in half to make two universities, one to continue as before, one to be subject to the legislature (that is, one provincial and one legislative). The Methodists and the Roman Catholics had secured legislative assent to colleges of their own in other towns, and Strachan had voted in council in their favour. He remained wedded to his original idea of one great provincial university on its magnificent site. Not for him the anomaly of a denominational college, or of a university subject to the whims of a chance majority in the Assembly. Yet in 1837, with many misgivings, he took a step that was ultimately to produce both. The college council surrendered its charter to be amended by the legislature. The judges of the King's Bench replaced the bishop of Quebec as visitor. The speakers of the legislature, the attorney general, and the solicitor general came onto the council. All religious tests save an admission of the Trinity disappeared. Nothing in fact was lost by any of the changes, and it would have been well if James Stephen had made them at the beginning. What was dangerous was the fact of surrender. What the legislature had been permitted to do once, to amend a royal charter, it could do at will again. Yet for the time being it appeared that the legislature could be trusted and that the province at large was safe.

John George Lambton, Earl of Durham, spent five months in the Canadas as governor general in 1838. Five days he spared for Niagara Falls, as if he were one more touring Englishman, one day only for Toronto. He was not to make his report until the following July, but rumours flooded the province. The overriding need was to settle the problem of the French. Upper Canada must be thrown into a union with them. It was the solution Strachan had opposed fifteen years before, and he liked it no better now.

In consequence, John Strachan set off for England that spring to be consecrated a bishop in the English succession with mixed feelings indeed. Upper Canada was to become a diocese at the very moment that it was ceasing to be an independent province. His parish church and proposed cathedral had burned to the ground. And to provide an anxiety overwhelming all others, Agnes, a precarious seventeen, was gravely ill with ever-recurring convulsions. He delayed his journey as long as he decently could, then borrowed funds as usual and started off with regret.

John Beverley Robinson took him in tow in England and his spirits revived. They visited every eminent physician and sent back new instructions and prescriptions for the girl to the Toronto doctors. They waited upon the crown lawyers and the archbishop. On the night of August 3 they went to a soirée at the home of Thomas Campbell in Lincoln's Inn. Campbell, being Scotch and a poet, must be seen on every trip home. "He proposed to drink 'to the memory of Archdeacon Strachan' who was to be consecrated bishop tomorrow. 'Come, come,' he said, 'doctor, don't go away. You're not a seceder, you're a churchman.' " Next day Strachan and Aubrey Spencer, first bishop of Newfoundland, were consecrated in the chapel of Lambeth Palace. Spencer was of the family of the Dukes of Marlborough. The colonials knew themselves to be in well-connected company. They dined with Archbishop Howley, toured the gardens and the library, and took their leave. "We thought little of this at Cornwall in 1806," said Robinson.[23]

23   Charles W. Robinson, *Life of Sir John Beverley Robinson* (Toronto: Morang, 1904), p. 290.

There were still the church societies to see, and Lord John Russell who became Colonial Secretary that month. John Henry Newman and Walter Hook, vicar of Leeds, Strachan tried to see without success. A hurried trip to Scotland took him to the bedside of his sister for a last farewell. As soon as possible he took ship for New York. Agnes was holding her own, as he left. On his arrival he was given word of her death. On Thursday, November 7, he came into Kingston and received the felicitations of the clergy. On the ninth he was at his house, the "episcopal palace" now, but the family so sadly diminished. One of Richard Cartwright's sons, the Reverend Robert, wrote him a note from Kingston: "I thought of you all day on Friday as you approached your home. I pray God to bless you ... Your Episcopate may be said to be sown in tears."[24]

There was one incidental advantage to being a bishop, that he could go no further. Robert Gourlay, years before, had made a telling point when he had said that Dr. Strachan had gone about blowing a trumpet before his charities. It was uncomfortably true. He had been realist enough as a youth to seek a patron above all other blessings. He had served with an awareness of the eye of authority ever since. It was the way the establishment worked. Appointments came from above, from governors, and back of them from the ever-changing colonial secretaries and the half dozen persons behind them. An earl's son like Charles James Stewart could rise above such considerations. A lowly born Scotchman in a remote colony could not. Until the last moment some Englishman could have been appointed bishop of Toronto, some friend of a passing minister, chosen with no more care for his suitability to

24   Henry Cartwright of Barriefield, Cartwright Papers, R. D. Cartwright to Strachan, 14 Nov. 1839.

office than the various judges and other functionaries that were foisted upon the colony. You therefore established your claim early, did your duty for the pleasure of it, but remained visible. It was at least no more degrading than serving the many-headed monster, democracy. You could say what should be said without worrying about public opinion. But it was still a price that had to be paid if you had opinions and wanted the opportunity to put them into practice, or if you were only one more Scotchman on the make. Now at the age of sixty-one he was free of that old preoccupation. There was nothing further that any minister could give John Strachan. His dependence could be upon Providence alone.

It was true that he must still work with the colonial secretaries and their appointees. He was disappointed in 1839 that Lord John Russell would not give St. James' Cathedral some grace from the Queen, but he had asked. He would still wrestle with governors and legislatures, with parliament itself even to the bishops who voted in the House of Lords. But all these strivings and arrangements would be for the benefit of the church, his duty to the diocese. It would take skill and much labour, but it could no longer be considered self-seeking, even by himself.

On December 22, 1839, Bishop Strachan had himself enthroned in his cathedral and parish church, the fourth St. James' that had been rising during his absence. He was now fully entered upon his labours.

Regrettably the first of these was the old business of the clergy reserves. Charles Poulett Thomson, the governor general, was in York persuading the legislature of Upper Canada to vote itself out of existence. As a preliminary, he was pushing through a bill to dispose of the clergy reserves. His solution was to sell them all, to fund the proceeds, and after allowing for vested interests to assign one-half of the revenue to be divided between the churches of England and Scotland according to their numbers, the other half among the remaining religious bodies. Strachan at once issued a circular letter to each congregation asking for petitions to the imperial government, while regretting that his first communication with them had to be concerned with such a subject. In the event, the imperial parliament passed its own Canada Clergy Act in August. All remaining reserves were to be sold but at a rate of no more than one hundred thousand acres a year. Of the income from sales prior to the passing of the Act, two-thirds would go to the Church of England, one-third to the Church of Scotland. Of the income from "new sales," one-third would go to the Church of England, one-sixth to the Scotch, the remainder to other religious bodies, should they accept it, or to the general cause of education. The church was guaranteed its present income of seventy-seven hundred pounds a year from other revenue if the Clergy Fund did not yield this income. To Strachan, the whole principle was wrong, since in the Act Britain appeared to recognize multiple establishments in a manner she would not do at home, but a final settlement was desirable, and laws must be obeyed. It was something that his labours, and his influence in Britain, had produced a larger proportion for the church than Thomson's bill envisaged.

Then, before the last session of the legislature ended, he produced a measure of his own. The Church Temporalities bill was an omnibus affair, providing for the rights of pewholders, the qualifications of churchwardens, the regulation of vestry meetings, but its principal object was to provide for the receiving of landed property by the church.

"I cannot think by what miracle this bill passed," wrote Robinson, "even in the last house, I am not sure I should consider it almost a recompense for the loss of our seven-twelfths of the Reserves."[25]

On that more promising note, the legislature of Upper Canada came to an end, and Strachan could turn to the main business of a diocesan bishop which must always be men and missions. On April 12, his sixty-second birthday, he laid hands on his first ordinands and sent them off to their parishes. Three were his own boys, Upper Canadians. Four were Britishers sent over by the societies. One was a Methodist from the Yonge Street circuit, conforming to the establishment. A month later he set off to visit the whole diocese himself.

It is the duty of a bishop to lay hands upon those who offer themselves and have been prepared for the rite of confirmation. English diocesans could content themselves with holding mass services in their cathedrals and principal churches. Mountain and Stewart had made visitation tours, usually at three-year intervals. Strachan believed that he must go to every mission and congregation in the country and lay his hands on the candidates before the altar at which they would normally worship. Where illness prevented them attending, he would confirm at the bedside. It followed that he must travel, over the whole diocese in 1840, over a third of it each succeeding year. The essence of travel was that it consumed time. Diarists and visitors might expatiate upon the awful roads, impossible in spring and fall, hot and dusty in summer. Every traveller had his tales of broken waggons and winded horses, of pot-holes, swamps, and corduroy roads. A seasoned and resourceful man could overcome anything and walk if necessary. Nothing could restore

25   John B. Robinson to Strachan, quoted in PAO, Strachan Letter Book to the Societies (henceforth SLB-SPG), p. 15, Strachan to Campbell, 20 Nov. 1840.

to him the hours spent moving from place to place. Strachan drew up a list of the appointments and published it in *The Church* – the Niagara District first, the Home and Simcoe Districts next, the eastward run, and then, wisely reserved for the cooler months, the London and Western Districts. The listings were inexorable, morning one mission, afternoon one or two more, day after day. He could conceive of this stretching on through the years that were left to him, exacting and unchanging, but knew too that it was the essential part of his duty. He must travel every road that his newest young ordinand travelled. He must encourage every congregation, speak to every child, sustain and question every clergyman, and reconnoitre each new township emerging from the bush and still destitute of the services of the church. He would incidentally note the housekeeping arrangements of the clergymen's wives, for the benefit of Ann, left alone in the Palace, but this they would not know. When all was done he must write up the journeys for the missionary societies, that they might know how their funds were spent, and the further needs.

The first year's visitation began on May 24 when Strachan stepped ashore at Niagara. It ended late in the fall when he came in by waggon from the west. Some of it was familiar. At Chippewa parsonage he dined with Margaret England, the girl who had jilted him thirty-seven years before, now married to her third husband, the rector. On Queenston Heights he stopped to see the ruins of the monument to Brock, blown up on the Good Friday before. In Picton, his old pupil from Cornwall days, William Macaulay, presented candidates and noted of his bishop that "he is in hale and stout health, but shows on his countenance and in his manner, the marks of age and the impression of care."[26] At

---

26 PAO, Macaulay Papers, William Macaulay to Ann Macaulay, 23 July 1840.

Goderich, he could be with Elizabeth and her husband and with Captain James who had turned from the army to law under the patronage of the Canada Company.

Britain had meanwhile created the Province of Canada out of the two former colonies, and Poulett Thomson, now Baron Sydenham of Sydenham and Toronto, was busy pulling together a governor's party of former tories and former reformers and new men on their way. The old politics and policies were presumably forgotten. Strachan had a vicarious entry into the new game. His son James did what the Constitutional Act had prohibited to him, he sought election to the legislature and won, even though his constituency returning officer was Sydenham's man. James sat through the three months of the first session of the first parliament in Kingston until a recount unseated him.

Lord Sydenham took a passing opportunity to mortify the bishop. In a despatch to Lord John Russell he noted that some of the King's College funds were in Strachan's hands for Strachan's private advantage, and questions were asked on the floor of the house. The bishop was outraged. He had borrowed from the funds to the amount of four thousand pounds, but it was ratified by a vote of the council and Sir George Arthur knew. The purpose of the endowments was to bring in income. The interest he paid was as good as any man's. He had borrowed money all his life, although hitherto privately, and had spent it without grudging, but now he was left with the reflection that it had been unwise to give the appearance of dabbling in public funds, and that Sydenham's system of "management" knew no limits.

Sydenham lay dying of tetanus in Kingston as Strachan took the next step in the organization of his diocese. He called the clergy together for a visitation in St. James' Cathedral and for one and a half hours read them his first episcopal charge. It was the usual affair, inherited through Mountain and Stewart from the English church. The clergy could consult one another. The bishop reviewed the state of the church at home and in the diocese and set their common labours in perspective. "Few of us, my brethren, may live to behold so blessed a consummation as the diocese studded over its whole surface with churches and pious congregations," he assumed, but all could so do their duty "that all blindness may be done away and every obstacle removed which in any way hinders our Catholic and Apostolic Church from receiving into her bosom the vast majority of our growing population."[27] But more than triennial visitations were necessary, however stately. The visitation must be turned in time into an annual meeting of clergy and laity deliberating together, as in the American church.

Strachan began now to create diocesan institutions, as Hobart had done. He already had a diocesan newspaper, *The Church*, edited by A. N. Bethune in Cobourg. He founded a Diocesan Theological Institute, again in Cobourg, a seminary in all but name where men could live and train together before ordination under Bethune's correct and diligent supervision. The most ambitious measure of all was the creation of a church society of the diocese of Toronto. There had long been district associations of the English church missionary societies and a Toronto-based Society for Converting and Civilizing the Indians and Propagating the Gospel among Destitute Settlers in Upper Canada. There was need for some organization to provide pensions to clergy

27 John Strachan, *A charge delivered to the clergy of the diocese of Toronto, at the primary visitation* ... (Toronto: Rowsell, 1841).

widows. Most of all, Strachan wanted to raise funds in Canada West to pay for new travelling missionaries. The answer seemed to be one omnibus church society combining all objects and all former societies, with branches in every district and parish. On to the central board of management came Robert Baldwin and William Henry Draper, political opponents though they were. The result was that the whole diocese appeared to be organized for its central missionary task, with room in the society for all godly causes in addition.

The greatest achievement of all was the opening of the University of King's College. On St. George's Day 1842 the governor general laid the cornerstone of the new building rising in university park, while the artillery fired salutes and the band of the 93rd played *Non Nobis Domine*. Afterwards in the hall of Upper Canada College there were toasts and speeches, Latin odes and Greek anacreontics, and a cold collation. Council and governor dined that night at the Palace and the college was launched in a happy union of church and state appetites. Twenty-six students registered in June of 1843, three professors arrived from England, and instruction commenced in the borrowed buildings of the legislature until the new one was ready. It was, said Strachan, the happiest moment of his life. The prime cause was the latest governor general, Sir Charles Bagot. Urbane and university-bred himself, he had the happiest of all connections in that his brother was the Bishop of Oxford. Bishop Bagot, indeed, had chosen the professors and had canvassed half a dozen rising Tractarian dons, William Palmer of Worcester among them, before securing a willing candidate for the divinity chair. King's College, as a provincial university, had an uncertain future, but at least it had begun well. Given quiet, it could go on to prove itself and win men's loyalty. Meanwhile for Strachan there were his travels, and the men and their missions.

One journey held elements of romance. The Superintendent of Indian Affairs went off to Manitoulin Island in 1842 where the wandering tribes were presumably becoming fixed, with the aid of an annual gift-giving ceremony, and Strachan chose to go with him. It gave evidence of the union of church and state and brought him to the missions under agreeable circumstances. The party set off from Penetanguishene in the old style, in canoes manned by Indian and Canadian voyageurs, the bishop in one canoe, a touring English lord in another. At nightfall, they pitched camp on convenient islands, had dinner around the camp-fires, prayers and hymns with the Christian Indians. One night it rained and Strachan spent it inside his leaking tent, his umbrella open above him. At Manitoulin, the mission was bright with promise; Sault Ste Marie was an all but deserted station. It would all make good reading for the societies, but Strachan was rueful about the time consumed and resolved to use steamboats in the future. One longer trip was saved him. He stood at the outlet of Lake Superior and considered how another time he could go on to Fort William and the Red River country. With some gratitude, he discovered next year that the gentle Bishop of Montreal was going instead at the request of the Hudson's Bay Company, and he could consider Sault Ste Marie the farthest bound of his responsibility.

The journeys repeated one another as year followed year. Wherever he lodged, he was up at five or six, wrote letters, ate an egg if possible, and was off in the waggon by seven. At the morning service he confirmed, addressed the candidates, preached, and moved on again for the next appointment at two or three (or two and four). Dinner came at night in a parsonage or an inn, conversation, prayers, a glass of milk, and bed at ten. Brown his verger went with him until Brown was too old. A parson usually travelled alongside, a chaplain for days at a time or the local missionary. Most of it was dull work, save for the company, "trundling along" in waggon or carriage. Side trips into Indian reserves on horseback or twelve miles in five hours through swamps made the dullness more acceptable. He used steamships wherever possible, entrusting himself to the lake he had formerly avoided. In the 'fifties, the "cars" were a major boon, bowling home along the Grand Trunk or the Great Western at admirable speeds and immune to weather. Whenever possible, he broke the journeys and came back for a few days with his wife and with his mail.

The mail was his other preoccupation. He saved everything that came to him, wrote first in a letter-book the draft of everything that went out. The great concern was men for the missions. Every year, by dint of much care, their numbers increased: clergy from England or Ireland, candidates from the societies, graduates of Bethune's teaching, and eventually (though briefly) men trained by the professor of divinity at King's. Dissensions in Canadian Methodism gave him a dozen candidates, despite his own deep suspicion that he was buying them. The Free Church disruption of the Church of Scotland brought him some pleasing recruits, although that pleasure was modified by regret for the disruption itself. As a Scotchman he wanted educated men, as a British American he needed self-reliant labourers. "A little Latin and the ability to ride a horse" became the basic credentials. Inevitably everything happened to them: travelling accidents and typhus, domestic tragedies and discouragements, the wastage of faction and party spirit. Strachan saw them in his study or on the visitation, poured forth in letter after letter encouragement, rebuke, money, and practical advice. It was the best fruit of being the man he was: that now, seasoned, ever sanguine, and eminently knowledgeable, he could be pastor to the clergy of Canada West.

Three incidents of the late 'forties may serve to indicate other facets of the bishop's personality.

Ernest Hawkins, secretary of the SPG, came out to the province in 1849 to see the needs for himself. Intelligent, observant, responsible for financing the church in half the colonies of the empire, he missed nothing. He disembarked at Kingston in August to find Strachan, fresh from a confirmation journey, ordaining 16 new deacons in the morning, confirming 136 persons at night, and presiding over a luncheon for 34 on the Monday. The bishop's manner, he noted, "is not good or impressive. His address afterwards, however, was warm, and in a manner eloquent." Two days later he dined in Toronto at the Palace. "The bishop's table was admirably ordered – the wines, even as critical as I am, remarked as being first rate."[28] Strachan valued a good table at the end of the day and what he termed "Social enjoyments."

In 1845 the bishop wrote four anonymous letters attacking Frederick Widder, commissioner of the Canada Company and a member of the council of the Church Society. The letters were delivered to A. N.

28   SPGA, Ernest Hawkins, "Manuscript journal of a tour in Canada and America, July–Nov. 1849."

Bethune by a theological student and inserted through an intermediary in a Hamilton newspaper under the pseudonym "Aliquis". They were a bitter, personal, public attack upon Widder's character, upon his "underhand working through the newspapers,"[29] and upon his lack of candour and integrity. The occasion was Widder's proposal to have the Canada Company named agent for the sale of the remaining clergy reserves, or if that failed, to have the Company manage the shares that might come to the Church Society or to others on a division. Neither alternative was ever likely of acceptance. In any event, the Church Society was Strachan's and would follow his lead. The anonymous attack was therefore unnecessary as well as risky. Thomas Mercer Jones, the other commissioner, who was in the know, could not but be embarrassed, although he and Widder were rivals. Strachan had simply never given up his undergraduate delight in anonymous cleverness and would go to any lengths, or depths, to pursue his scheme of the moment.

On April 6, 1849, a great fire raged through the city of Toronto. Strachan went to bed confident that St. James' was safe, being built entirely of stone. Should the wind change, the Palace had the protection of its walled garden. At four in the morning he was awakened by a man who had crawled over the wall to report that the cathedral was in danger. Burning shingles had been dashed up into the open louvres of the steeple and it was afire. There was time to take out everything movable, but the firemen were engaged elsewhere and Strachan had to stand by and watch the building burn. Those who saw him observed that he whistled mournfully as he stood. The cathedral of his enthronement and of his rectorship was no more.

29 Aliquis [John Strachan], *Observations on the history and recent proceedings of the Canada company; addressed in four letters to Frederick Widder, esq. ...* (Hamilton, 1845), p. 53. Cf. Alan Wilson, *The Clergy Reserves of Upper Canada* (Toronto: University of Toronto Press, 1968), chap. XII.

Separations and Unions

As the eighteen-forties wore away, so too did the hope of maintaining the connection between church and state. Strachan would fight for it to the end, but that end was ever coming into view.

First to go was the University of King's College. No session of the Canadian parliament passed without some legislation being introduced threatening change. Robert Baldwin proposed a University of Toronto with King's, Regiopolis, Victoria, and Queen's as subordinate colleges, but then went out of office. His successor, W. H. Draper, proposed the University of Upper Canada on substantially the same lines in 1845 and again in 1846 with no more success. The sinuous John A. Macdonald brought in a bill in 1847 that would have given King's its 1827 charter, its site, and an income of three thousand pounds a year. The remaining proceeds of the endowment, estimated at seven thousand pounds, were to be divided among the other colleges, among the district grammar schools, among new model agricultural farms, and for general education. What is more, Macdonald believed that he had the Bishop's consent.

Strachan was in some difficulty. The site and three thousand a year until the next division of funds might have saved King's for the church, but the charter of 1827 was not, in fact, the charter of a denominational college, however much others might think so. The governor was chancellor, which in these days of responsible government meant the ministry. Moreover Strachan was as committed as Baldwin by now to the old hope of one great provincial university situated in that magnificent Toronto park and sustained by an undivided endowment. The question was perhaps immaterial. John A. Macdonald in later years was to remark to his secretary "that no man had ever been more unduly lauded than Bishop Strachan, whose obstinacy did more harm to the Church of England than anything else." "The Church," he said, "lost every sixpence in consequence."[1] In fact, the tottering ministry withdrew its university bills, went to the country, and was soundly beaten. Baldwin and LaFontaine came in once more, each with an assured majority. Strachan called upon his old pupil and in an hour's discussion learned the fate of the university he had founded. King's was to become the University of Toronto, site, endowment, and all. Divinity would be eliminated. The church had no part in the provincial university.

Strachan knew what he had to do. The church must have a college even as the Methodists and the Church of Scotland had, a place to train clergy if nothing else. The Earl of Elgin tactfully suggested a divinity professorship attached to the cathedral, "or some other arrangement which may better approve itself to your judgment,"[2] and offered a personal subscription. But Strachan had his plans laid long since. The Cobourg Theological Institute should be moved up to Toronto, turned into a college, say Trinity College, and endowed from the mounting clergy reserve funds. It would train clergy. It could be expanded to teach undergraduates, as Queen's and Victoria did. The deterrent had been King's. To start another college would indicate that the church had given up the provincial university. Attorney General Sherwood had offered him an act of incorporation in 1847, but the time was not yet. Once King's was gone, the way was clear. The church could be said to have been despoiled. The University of Toronto was unequivocally secular. The ministry, dominated in Strachan's opinion by French Cana-

1 Joseph Pope, *Memoirs of the Right Honourable Sir John A. Macdonald* (2 vols.; Ottawa: J. Durie, 1895), p. 54.
2 Strachan Papers, Elgin to Strachan, 6 Nov. 1849.

dians despite its reform majority from Canada West, had broken with British educational tradition. Britain could hardly refuse to make good the loss.

Strachan mounted a major campaign. He collected twenty-five thousand pounds in Canada, much of it admittedly prospective. The list of subscribers reads like an index to his life: boys from the Cornwall school, parishioners of York, names from the travelling missions. Then in April of 1850, two days before his seventy-second birthday, he set off for England by way of New York, carrying with him petitions to the Queen and to the two houses of parliament, as weapons to be used if necessary. His reception was all that could be desired. Sir John Colborne, now Baron Seaton, came on to a committee that met every Wednesday to direct the campaign. W. E. Gladstone attended, and the aged Duke of Wellington, who agreed to turn over his Toronto property to the church college and promised a further donation. Strachan waited twice upon Sir Robert Peel, and though the former prime minister died suddenly before a third appointment, Strachan could claim his posthumous assistance in a printed memoir of the interviews. Lord Grey in the Colonial Office was the principal object of attention. He refused to permit a donation from the Queen to head the lists or a Queen's letter to authorize collections in all the parish churches, but he saw no reason why a royal charter should not be granted, subject to advice from the governor general of Canada. The charter, in fact, would be the chief difficulty. Strachan had pointed out to Sir Robert Peel that it was hardly wise to leave the granting to "our enemies" at home. Grey picked up the phrase as if it applied to the governor general and gave Strachan the opportunity to reply: "That lamented statesman knew as well as I did that the words 'our enemies' do not include or apply to the Earl of Elgin, who is not believed to be clothed with sufficient authority to intervene with effect under what is called Responsible Government."[3] In fact both Grey and Elgin wanted the charter settled quickly and amicably. They had an English clergy reserves bill in prospect and wanted no additional occasion of alarm. The decision was not theirs to make. Whether the Queen granted, or did not grant, to the Church of England a university charter equal to those already given to the Church of Scotland, the Methodists, and the Roman Catholics, must rest with Robert Baldwin and Louis LaFontaine.

Strachan meanwhile toured Britain for what might well be the last time. There were journeys to Edinburgh, through Yorkshire to Liverpool, back to Glasgow and Edinburgh again, down through the Isle of Wight, the bishop speaking and presenting his case as often as opportunity offered. In October he sailed for home on the steamship *Canada*, which incidentally ran on the rocks thirty miles out of Halifax. He had collected fifteen thousand pounds with the promise of more.

Back in Toronto a substantial Church University Board had been gathered together and there were decisions to be made. The University of Trinity College would be built in Toronto rather than on sites offered in Niagara and Hamilton. The building would be modelled on plans for St. Aidan's College, Birkenhead, plans brought back by the bishop. The site would be a repetition of King's College, only twenty acres this time, but on Queen Street to the northwest of the city, facing the bay, with yet another creek running through the property, Garrison

3   *Ibid.*, Strachan to Grey, 17 July 1850 (quoted under date of 5 June 1851).

Creek in place of the Taddle. Professors were imported from Oxford and Cambridge as before, through the SPG rather than Bishop Bagot of Oxford. Funds were smaller, but the process was the same, and this time there were no delays. The first sod was turned by Strachan in March of 1851; on April 30 the cornerstone was laid with ceremony, the clergy and lay representatives of the diocese being present in force for what was to be the first synod on the morrow. In January of 1852 the first students came up from Cobourg and lectures began.

Robert Baldwin conceded the charter in 1851. He had wanted but one university in his beloved Toronto and had hoped that Queen's and Victoria would surrender their charters in arts. When they finally refused, he gave in. The University of Toronto had thirty-three matriculated students in all years in the fall of 1852. Trinity matriculated twenty-one, apart from divinity men, when it opened. Such numbers would not warrant two institutions but the logic of secularization had brought it about. An act of incorporation went through the legislature that summer of Baldwin's ministry with his active assistance (and with a resurrected William Lyon Mackenzie hotly opposed), and the royal charter followed in 1852.

The end of King's College suggested a kindred reform, the secularization of the clergy reserves. The settlement of 1841 had presumably been final, but finality was hardly to be expected in the changing colonial condition. Strachan himself had been petitioning for changes since 1843. He asked that the church's share of the endowments be transferred out of the public domain into the hands of the Church Society, shrewdly believing that only then could they be permanent. Balked in this, he protested at regular intervals against the heavy expenses of management by the officers of the commissioner of crown lands. Five clergy went without salary for two years and further appointments were delayed when the income dropped below the guarantee of seventy-seven hundred pounds a year and each government left it to the other to assume responsibility for the guarantee. Finally the income from new sales restored the deficit and an ever-mounting surplus seemed assured. From 1847 onwards Strachan had funds at his disposal, subject only to the advice of the Society for the Propagation of the Gospel. New missions took precedence and a fund for widows, but much could be done with little and even new bishoprics were a possibility. A brief rebellion flared up among a group of his clergy led by Benjamin Cronyn of London. They assumed that rising reserve funds should mean rising salaries for themselves from those funds. Strachan was realist enough by now to believe that parochial endowments were only effective at a level that guaranteed subsistence. Useful clergy were more apt to remain so if they were in part dependent upon voluntary local support. He would use the money for new ventures at his own discretion until the time came to lay down his authority.[4]

Regrettably the rise in income from the reserve funds contributed to their end. The Canada Clergy Act of 1841 had assigned half of the proceeds of new sales to other religious bodies or to general purposes as the legislature might decide. Not until 1847 was there any appreciable sum to be disposed of and no decision had been necessary. The new surplus provoked heart-searching. To the voluntarist, religion must be self-sustaining, untrammelled by state aid or state interference. More-

4   John Strachan, *Secular State of the Church* ... (Toronto: Diocesan Press, [1849]).

over most of the Upper Canadian Scotch had gone out of the Church of Scotland in the disruption of 1843 and 1844 and now took their stand against establishments. In all good conscience, they and the others must refuse to share in the funds now so embarrassingly available. Nor was Strachan's oft repeated and only half ironical compromise a continuing possibility: let each body choose, he said, according to its principles, the voluntarists to refuse funds, the establishment to take them. Given the power, the reformers of Canada West would secularize all the reserves, and power was theirs after 1848.

The next obstacle was the British act. Any change in the existing arrangements had to be made by the imperial parliament and Canadian politicians found themselves frustrated in a matter they considered to be of purely domestic interest. Baldwin and LaFontaine may have had no wish to disturb religious endowments, but it was galling to them and to their followers that the power to do so was denied them. And, inevitably, all sorts of irresponsible solutions could be advanced on the hustings under cover of that powerlessness, and the question thus became one more test of self-government. A formal request for enabling legislation was made to Britain in June of 1850. During two successive British administrations the request was abortive. Grey proposed to attempt a bill, but his time ran out. His successor, Sir John Pakington, wrote that Her Majesty's Government "could only regard any measure which would place it in the power of any accidental majority in the Colonial Legislature, however small, to divert forever from its sacred object the funds ... set aside for the religious instruction of the people, with the most serious doubt."[5] Then, in December 1852, Aberdeen's

5   Strachan Papers, Pakington to Hincks, 1852.

ministry replaced Lord Derby's and a Canadian Clergy Reserve bill was at once introduced.

Strachan felt himself too old and too suspect to undertake the defence in England. Bishop Mountain of Quebec went over, and Archdeacon Bethune. The fight was lost before it began. Gladstone would not shrink away from any trouble to serve "the good and manful Bishop of Toronto,"[6] but liberal principles required that colonies have power over their domestic arrangements. In the House of Lords, nine bishops led by Samuel Wilberforce voted for the bill, and Strachan felt that the English church had betrayed him. One important point was conceded. The British had characteristically safeguarded vested interests and all existing salaries and payments were guaranteed for life.

The field of battle shifted once more to Canada. The ministry, now under Hincks and Morin, found their new power an embarrassment and in the confusion of parties could produce no acceptable solution as the election of 1854 approached. Strachan poured forth a storm of letters and pamphlets demonstrating the validity of establishments and the claims of the church in Canada, but at the same time he made sure that as many of the younger clergy as possible were on the funds. His son, Captain James, produced a further series of papers recommending a compromise division of the funds among the churches. In the end, the reserves were to play their part in making a new Canadian political party. Under the guidance of John A. Macdonald, the moderate conservatives went into the election of 1854 with secularization an open question. After the election and the defeat of the government, they entered into an alliance with the French wing of the ministry and with

6 SPGA, Hawkins to Strachan, quoting Gladstone, 28 March 1851.

some of the reformers in a new Liberal-Conservative coalition. The Upper Canadian radicals had been shut out, and on October 17, Macdonald himself produced a bill to secularize.

Macdonald's bill declared that it was desirable to remove all semblance of connection between church and state and was regarded as so doing. Whether, in fact, the bill did so or not, it was clearly a defeat of the first magnitude for the idea of a national church. John Strachan's long struggle to maintain the establishment was at an end. The principle, so often advanced and as often compromised, was now finally repudiated, and at the hands of a ministry that included the church's friends. But if the principle was lost, the money was still available. The bill set up two municipalities funds, one east, one west, and vested in them the proceeds of the reserves. Clause two provided that, as the British act required, the stipends now being paid to the clergy should be a first charge upon the funds for their natural lives or incumbencies. And because such a charge would sew up a major portion of the funds for years, clause three permitted a commutation of the annual salaries and allowances for lump sums.[7]

There were thus two alternatives for Strachan. Either he and his clergy continued to receive their salaries until they died, when the funds ceased, or the men could commute for a sum based on each life expectancy, the monies could be funded into one capital account in the hands of the Church Society and the Society could thereafter be responsible for paying the men. There were difficulties to be seen at every turn. The men might not wish to commute, content to remain stipendiaries of

7 *Statutes of the Province of Canada passed in the Eighteenth Year of the Reign of Her Majesty Queen Victoria* (Quebec, 1854), pp. 7–8, as quoted in John Moir, *Church and State in Canada, 1627–1867* (Toronto: McClelland and Stewart, 1967), pp. 243–5. John Moir, *Church and State in Canada West* (Toronto: University of Toronto Press, 1959), chap. III, discusses the commutation.

the state rather than of the church. The commutation funds might not be sufficient to bear the charges upon them, and indeed in theory should not be, without consuming the capital. Finally, the act had set a term of twelve months to the right to commute. On the other hand, Strachan had been pleading since 1819 to have the clergy reserves taken out of the public domain and handed over to the church for whose benefit presumably they were intended, and here at last was the opportunity. Indeed Francis Hincks was to say later that secularization with commutation had been undertaken upon Strachan's initiative.[8] There could be no doubt that it was to the church's advantage.

A sustained round of activity ensued. John Hillyard Cameron, a member of the government if not of the ministry, and solicitor and trustee for the Church Society, conducted the negotiations from both sides in Quebec, the then seat of government. Strachan dealt with the clergy. Some signed readily, but every kind of scruple had to be met and he could only sympathize and raise new arguments. Men who believed in a state church and state support had reason to demur at being paid by a diocesan who admitted that the funds might be inadequate. It was a tribute to their loyalty and to their good sense that they signed in time, with perhaps some assistance from the radicals in the House who began to take note that secularization by the MacNab-Morin ministry was not spoliation but a division of the funds. The next step was to invest the capital, and again it was Cameron's skill in an investor's market that was called upon. The government was as generous as the legislation permitted. The SPG contributed seventy-five hundred pounds towards capital. Some clergy commuted who had remained upon the diocesan

8 Francis Hincks, *Religious Endowments in Canada* (London: Dalton and Lucy, 1869), p. 102.

lists only long enough to do so and never drew upon the funds. In the end it was discovered that there was in fact no deficiency. A capital sum had been realized, the income from which was sufficient to meet all existing demands.

The secularization of the clergy reserves still marked the end of an era. The idea of an establishment had been abandoned, and of more practical moment, the years of steady expansion supported by the proceeds of new sales were over. New missions after this must be undertaken with private funds, if at all. But the church retained a reasonable share of her patrimony from the Constitutional Act, and had it in her own hands; Strachan could rest content that he had fought effectively.

The preamble of Macdonald's Act provoked Strachan's wry disdain, declaring as it did the separation of church and state. The church in Canada, declared the bishop to his visitation of 1856, "has connections with the Mother Church and the Constitution of the Empire which the Colonial authorities are incompetent to dissolve. ... Though we have been made independent as it were by violence, the act affects nothing more than our connection with the Colonial government."[9] The next task was to free the church to govern herself and to turn the discarded establishment into an independent denomination.

Strachan had come to the basic answers long ago when he had been archdeacon of York. The model would still be Bishop Hobart and the episcopal church in America. Let the church adopt conventions of clergy and lay representatives and speak with a united voice. In 1839 he had canvassed the law officers of the crown and other English churchmen and found them uniformly dissuasive. A convention would have

9   John Strachan, *A charge delivered to the clergy of the diocese of Toronto, at the visitation ... 1856* (Toronto: Rowsell, 1856), p. 5.

nothing to discuss, the laity had nothing to contribute, the clergy should stay at work in their parishes, authority resided in the bishop and in those who had appointed him. Instead, Strachan had founded the Church Society to meet some of the needs as a triennial visitation met others. At both the bishop presided with unquestioned power. But who was to appoint future bishops, his own replacement on his death or the men for the new dioceses that should soon be carved out of Toronto? As he trundled ever further along these roads, now in his seventies, the problem continued to obtrude itself.

Bishops normally were appointed by letters patent from the Queen, which meant the current British prime minister with some counsel from the Archbishop of Canterbury and the societies. In these days of responsible government it could mean the Canadian ministry. Briefly there had been the possibility of additional appointments to be supported by the colonial bishoprics fund that had given a bishop to New Brunswick in 1845. More briefly still, Strachan and Hawkins of the SPG had discussed names of persons for English appointments to Upper Canada paid for out of the clergy reserves surplus. With such dreams over, there remained only the prospect of locally raised endowments with the inescapable corollary of locally elected bishops. It was not a development the English church would relish. The first step, in any event, must be functioning synods, fully representative of the church in the diocese, meeting under the authority of a parliamentary enactment.

Once more John Strachan found himself negotiating on two fronts at once, and doing so amid all the distractions afforded by King's and

Trinity, secularization and commutation, and always the unremitting duty of the confirmation journeys. The visitation in Toronto must be carefully transformed into a synod while the prerequisite authority had to be won from England.

Fortunately every diocese in the colonial empire faced similar problems, although none had so large a church population as Toronto. The bishops found a common champion in Gladstone. He collected briefs from Strachan and others, consulted whom he could, and introduced a Colonial Church bill into the House of Commons, a bill "to relieve bishops in the colonies in respect to legal doubts and disabilities affecting the management of their church affairs" and to provide a common pattern of church government. The bill had to be withdrawn, and a second attempt in 1853 met with no more success. The Colonial Secretary had to warn his governors that imperial legislation appeared to be impossible and that they must try their own legislatures, but when the Australian bishops forthwith succeeded in getting a bill passed in the colony of Victoria, it was reserved as infringing upon the Queen's prerogative. Strachan watched the process with some irritation, scenting the opposition of dissenters and the pedantry of crown lawyers. He procured a copy of the Victoria bill, drew up his own for Canada, and sent it on to the bishops of Montreal and Quebec. They recommended conferences upon it and close study in each diocese, and Strachan saw the years passing by. Instead he closeted himself with John Hillyard Cameron and produced a short bill of two clauses. Clause one read: "The bishops, clergy, and laity ... may meet in their several dioceses, which are now or may be hereafter constituted in this province, and in such manner and by such proceedings as they shall adopt frame constitutions and make regulations for enforcing discipline in the Church, for the appointment, deposition, deprivation, or removal of any person bearing office therein, of whatever order or degree, any rights of the Crown to the contrary notwithstanding."[10] Clause two authorized a general assembly of all the dioceses within the province of Canada. The help of Peter Boyle de Blaquiere was enlisted, even though he had been the first chancellor of the University of Toronto, and he presented it to the Legislative Council where it passed unanimously. The Legislative Assembly had it in May and June of 1856, during a lull in the Grand Trunk debates, and the bill passed its second and third readings in one day. Strachan was quietly jubilant as he sent a copy of the proposed bill to his brother bishops in May, the completed Act in June. Sir Edmund Head, the governor general, reserved it for the Queen's pleasure, as was to be expected. The church in the province must wait once more upon the lawyers, but at least church and state in Canada had spoken with one voice.

Meanwhile Strachan had already fashioned his synod in all but law. For the fourth visitation of 1851 he directed his clergy to have each parish elect a lay representative and to bring them along to the visitation. There were other purposes in Strachan's mind, of course. The formal gathering was the day after the laying of the cornerstone of the University of Trinity College, and it was well that the church should be present in force. And amidst the threats to the clergy reserves some demonstration was desirable. "The Bishop," wrote Lord Elgin, "has called a sort of convention of his church. ... We shall see what views

---

10 Great Britain, *Parliamentary Papers*, 1857, C. 2256, pp. 3–4, 19 & 20 Vic., c. 141, as quoted in Moir, *Church and State in Canada*, p. 263.

they take of their interest; whether they are for compromise or for war to the knife."[11] On May the first in Holy Trinity Church (for St. James' was still in ruins), Strachan celebrated communion and made his usual visitation address. Afterwards the laity gave in their certificates of election and the gathering met at once, the clergy in their gowns on the right side, the laymen on the left. Strachan carefully sketched his terms: "In all diocesan meetings of the clergy over which the Bishop presides, no proceedings shall be introduced without his previous sanction, nor be considered carried without his approval." He then proposed the business of the meeting. "Shall we, the Church of the Diocese of Toronto, take any steps to protect her property and endowments? Shall we ... apply for permission from the Crown to hold Diocesan Synods or Convocations?"[12]

On the following day, the men debated, and amid a flurry of respectful resolutions produced the two that were necessary, one to be given self-government, another to retain the reserves. Strangely, that on the inviolability of the reserves settlement was proposed by the representative from Christ's Church, Hamilton, Sir Allan MacNab. It was at least gratifying that old George Okill Stuart should briefly preside at the end to put another, "that the thanks of this meeting are justly due and are hereby most cordially tendered to the Lord Bishop of Toronto for the extraordinary degree of zeal and energy which he has manifested ..."[13]

This was clearly not a synod, although the diocese was later to number it as the first, but the die had been cast. There could be no going

11   Arthur G. Doughty, ed., *The Elgin-Grey Papers, 1846–1852* (Ottawa: King's Printer, 1937), p. 820, Elgin to Grey, 23 April 1851.
12   "Minutes of Proceedings at the visitation of the Lord Bishop of Toronto," appended to John Strachan, *A charge delivered to the clergy of the diocese of Toronto, in May, MDCCCLI* (Toronto: Diocesan Press, 1851), pp. 54–60.
13   *Ibid.*

back to the purely clerical. There was some danger that the introduction of debate, even more than the presence of the laity, might open the way to party politics. The agitation over the clergy reserves surplus had been a warning. Lord Elgin reported darkly that it was all part of a movement to curb the power of the bishop.[14] Strachan knew the temptations, and the possibilities, and would make no mistakes.

The fifth visitation took place in October of 1853, delayed from the spring in the hope that Gladstone's bill would have passed. Instead, Macdonald's bill to secularize was only five days off, as some of the members well knew. One further step was taken. The assembly declared itself to be in fact a synod and appointed a committee to prepare a constitution and canons. An eager layman would have called it a standing committee, but this Strachan would not have. "The Bishop expressed his opinion that ... as to the Standing Committees in the United States, they did not meet his approval, because they encroached on the Bishop's rightful authority."[15]

Strachan retired to his library and worked out the constitution that he wanted. Letters came in from the American bishops, from his colleagues in Canada East, and from England. The Canadian pattern of church government would be a compromise, a conservative variant of the American. The bishop would have a veto over all legislation, although it would not be called such. Rather the agreement of each of the three orders, clergy, laity, and bishop would be necessary. To Strachan's mind, a synod must be a bishop and his men. If the bishop could be overruled it would mean in effect "reducing the bishop to a presbyterian

14   Doughty, ed., *Elgin-Grey Papers*, p. 641, Elgin to Grey, 3 May 1850.
15   Anglican Church of Canada, Dioceses, Toronto, *Triennial visitation of the Lord Bishop of Toronto, and proceedings of the church synod of the diocese of Toronto* ... (Toronto: Rowsell, 1853), p. 5.

moderator." "This," said Strachan, "will not happen in my time."[16] The third synod took place in October 1854, no longer even a semblance of a visitation for only a year had passed. The principal items of business were a declaration of principles upon which they meant to proceed and the passing of the constitution, confirmed at the fourth synod of May 1856. The pattern was set.

Royal assent to the Canadian Church bill, when it came in the spring of 1857, was something of an anticlimax except for one circumstance. An extra-legal election was in the offing. The Colonial Secretary wrote on April 3 that the Judicial Committee of the Privy Council had agreed. Sir Edmund Head gave the formal assent on May 27. Within six weeks John Strachan was presiding at the first episcopal election in the English church, and doing so backed by Legislative authority.

Sub-dividing a diocese and appointing a new bishop thereto was a notoriously difficult undertaking, as Strachan knew from his own case, but the *sine qua non* was money. It was perhaps as well that Canada West should speak with but one episcopal voice, his own, while the great projects of Trinity and the reserves and the synod went forward. For the lengthening confirmation journeys and the care of all the churches more bishops were necessary. As early as 1851, when the clergy reserve surplus might have paid for them, he had worked out the divisions he wanted, three equal areas in the south divided by the great river lines of the Trent and the Grand, one in the north and west for the Indian missions which he would call St. Mary. London and Kingston could become see cities, although their names were already in use elsewhere.

In January 1854 he took the plunge and issued a pastoral letter

---

16   Strachan Letter Book, 1854–62 (SLB 1854–62), p. 91, Strachan to Hibbert Binney, Oct. 1855.

seeking the funds from the people of Canada West. It followed, of course, that if the dioceses-to-be raised their own endowments, they should also choose their own bishops, from their own numbers if they wished, which meant episcopal elections by clergy and laity. There was no guarantee that the English church would concede so grave a novelty, but elections were implicit in the bill he and Cameron had prepared. Strachan had to persuade his canvassers to go ahead in faith, and at the same time to press the case upon England. Permission came in characteristically guarded manner from one of the five colonial secretaries of 1855. "Her Majesty's government are prepared to take the necessary steps ... whenever required to do so," wrote Sir William Molesworth to his governor general, "and that they will recommend to Her Majesty for appointment to the new bishopric such clergymen as you may yourself designate to them after consulting with the bishop and such other authorities of the Church of England in the colony as you may think advisable."[17] Strachan called upon Sir Edmund Head and found that gentleman prepared to place the happiest of constructions upon the despatch. The Queen would appoint, of course; Head would designate; the synod might elect. Only the assurance of an adequate endowment was necessary. Strachan had no need to worry about the west. Benjamin Cronyn of London, at the head of a phalanx of Irish clergy, was out collecting with a godly zeal. The east hung back, lacking such bold and interested leadership. The Toronto fund languished entirely, for all men could see that John Strachan was an unchanging permanency.

Strachan chose the name Huron for the new diocese, after the lake and the Indians who had roamed its shores. He had long since chosen

17 Quoted in *ibid.*, p. 104, Strachan to Cronyn, 28 Nov. 1855.

the bishop, Alexander Neil Bethune, archdeacon of York. The archdeacon demurred, sensing as well as his teacher that circumstances had
already given the post to Cronyn, but Strachan demanded that the
attempt be made. Bethune was a third-generation Canadian, scholarly
and correct. "I have said nothing of the good that you would do the
church in preventing Dr. Cronyn from becoming bishop, who though I
believe well-intentioned, is not qualified for the office and whose low
views are calculated to lower the church."[18] Briefly he considered pack-
ing the clerical electorate, but in the end chose to take no active part.
The members of synod for the western portion of the diocese of
Toronto met in St. Paul's Church, London, on the ninth of July.
Strachan delivered a solemn charge. An English clergyman preached
on the text "Thou Lord, which knowest the hearts of all men, shew
whether of these two men thou hast chosen," and the men voted as a
previous analysis had shown that they would, twenty-two clerical and
twenty-three lay votes for Cronyn, twenty clerical and ten lay for
Bethune. Bethune moved that the vote be made unanimous, Strachan
advised Head, Head recommended to the Colonial Secretary, and from
Osborne on the Isle of Wight Queen Victoria wrote "The Queen ...
approves of the appointment ... of Dr. Cronin [sic] as Bishop of Huron
in Canada."[19]

Back in his study, Strachan was warmed by Hawkins' approval. "I
make no observation on the particular selection made," he wrote, "but
speak only of the great fact that the Episcopate has been extended –
and a bishop chosen by the free votes of the clergy and laity. The
step is one of vast importance and one that must be followed in

18   SLB 1854–62, p. 207, Strachan to Bethune, 2 June 1857, first draft.
19   Huron College, Cronyn Papers, Victoria to Labouchere, 17 Aug. 1857.

the other colonies – and then – tho' not immediately – in England."[20]

John Strachan needed the support of his friends. His world as much as his diocese was shrinking. Synods and new dioceses might be tributes to his energy as well as the marks of a developing church, but in this eightieth year of his life much of the satisfaction was missing. Depression lay upon the province after the Crimean War and railway booms. Parishes were vacant and many of the clergy were unpaid, especially those unprotected by the commutation funds. The episcopal endowment in the east had come to a full stop, the clergy having wasted the good years in strange quarrels including a plan by Francis Hincks' friends to buy the bishopric for Hincks' brother. Most of all, Strachan suffered personal loss in his own family. John died in 1856, his affairs in disorder. John's only son, George, died six months later. In the spring of 1857 a hurried call brought him to the bedside of Elizabeth in Goderich. Her health had long been a matter of anxiety. Her death removed her mother's chief joy and support. There remained only Captain James in Toronto and the healthy Alexander in New York. Then in 1859 came a telegram to say that Alex had died. Ann Strachan was never the same again. She grieved for her departed family, seldom went out, soon seldom came downstairs. Strachan did what he could, remained home when his schedule permitted, and on the inexorable round wrote her daily before breakfast letters full of reminiscence and encouragement. "You have a natural inclination for order and regularity – and I have some also, but I do not know that I keep it up as well. I think the palace is a model of comfort and neatness, but not of splendour and luxury. It is fresh, tidy and airy, and the snuggest house

20   SPGA, Hawkins to Strachan, private, 31 July 1857.

that I know – good sense and good taste preside over all the arrangements. ... God bless you and keep you and give you health and strength."[21]

His own health largely held. His eyesight was dimming, there was the apprehension of deafness, lumbago plagued him occasionally as it had from his middle years. His appetite for work lessened, but he still came downstairs shaven to consume an egg and a roll and tea for breakfast at 8:30, to work in the library from 9:30 until six. Still he dressed for dinner, which remained an affair of some state, and then to bed at ten. There was no thought of retirement. He hoped to die in harness, to leave his wife to the care of John Beverley Robinson and of James. Meanwhile there remained two projects to round off his labours, the completion of the eastern diocese and the creation of a provincial synod.

The eastern endowment fund revived when Huron's success showed that it was possible. Again Strachan wanted Bethune to be elected and this time he did manage appointments with a view to helping his candidate. The east however had found its man in young John Travers Lewis, rector of Brockville, and Bethune withdrew before the election in 1861.

A provincial synod had been provided for by Strachan's Canadian legislation of 1856. It remained to persuade the bishops and their dioceses. Strachan sketched his plan, a house of clerical and lay representatives and a house of bishops meeting under "our Primus, the bishop of Quebec"[22] as metropolitan. "Primus," like "synod," was the term in use in the Scotch Episcopal Church. The means thereto would be the old one, petitions from the dioceses to the Queen through the Colonial Secretary. Huron under Benjamin Cronyn's direction refused

21 Strachan Papers, Strachan to Ann Strachan, 22 July 1851.
22 SLB 1854–62, p. 288, 26 March 1859.

to petition. Cronyn was content to be under the distant jurisdiction of Canterbury, prepared to keep his diocese an island of evangelical purity. To Strachan, provincial synods would be the necessary safeguard against such independence. In 1860 the Queen named the bishop of Montreal, Francis Fulford, to be metropolitan for the province of Canada. In September of 1861 the provincial synod met for the first time, in Montreal, Fulford presiding and responsible, the aged Strachan and Mountain feeling the passage of time, Cronyn present but suspicious, and with Travers Lewis, his consecration delayed, acting as secretary. Strachan drove around the city he had first come to sixty-two years before, and duly admired, and described for Ann's benefit, the prodigious new railway bridge across the river.

In the following March, Strachan went down to Kingston for his last official act there. John Travers Lewis was to be consecrated in Canada by his metropolitan, whereas all his predecessors had gone home to England. There, in St. George's Church, in the stone city of his first ambition, Strachan laid his hands upon the head of the young Irishman. The next bishop to be consecrated should be for Toronto.

There was now nothing remaining to prevent Strachan from laying down his office save Strachan himself. He held on. No bishop in Canada had as yet resigned while life was in him. The path of duty should be walked to the end. There was a Toronto episcopal fund to be collected. Bethune, already twice rejected, might not be elected by a Toronto synod, and Bethune was making the small decisions and handling much of the correspondence of the see. Most of all, Strachan recognized his own tenacity and would keep to his work, although he had come to dread the confirmation journeys. The trains helped. Confirmations near Hamilton were combined with weekends at F. L. Osler's parsonage in Dundas. Cobourg served as headquarters in the east. A journey to Sault Ste Marie was accomplished by means of the Northern Railway to Collingwood with John Beverley Robinson for company, and a steamboat ride to the Sault. Otherwise the regimen remained the same: breakfast at eight, two, three, and four services in a day, dinner as late as nine at night. It was at least a satisfaction to be accompanied by a Cartwright again, the Reverend Conway, son to Robert, grandson to Richard, his patron and friend.

More and more he was content to stay at home, working at some small project in his study, seeing his wife in her room. "We have been to one another after fifty years as at first," he wrote to a brother bishop. Mrs. Sibbald of Lake Simcoe would call upon him annually upon April the twelfth. "When shown into the library there sat the Bishop in an armchair with a tabby cat as big as a dog on his knee, the beast's two fore paws nearly reaching the Bishop's chin and the head resting on the paws." And in 1862 she noted, "He was in good spirits, but looked thin and worn, always with pen and ink before him ... He is beginning to stoop very much, he walks slower, and is getting deaf and blind, poor dear old man, he still chuckles and laughs, especially with Susie."[23]

There were some compensations in being old. He knew himself to be something of a historic personage in Toronto. His short, sturdy figure, clothed in the knee breeches and gaiters and frock coat of his order, was noted with favour on the city streets. They cheered him at the station when he went to say good-bye to Queen Victoria's son, the visiting

23   Francis Paget Hett, ed., *Memoirs of Susan Sibbald* (New York: Minton, Balch, 1926), pp. 317, 319–20.

Prince of Wales. He whistled Scots airs as he walked, or as he sat in his place in St. James', and recked not that what was a low murmur to him might be more audible to others. And there were still projects. He continued to press for a diocese of St. Mary, the last link in a chain of dioceses binding together British North America, and he badgered the societies for the funds for a mission at Sault Ste Marie as a first step. Canadian politics he watched with a knowing interest and waited for the break-up of the union he disliked, for the freeing of Canada West and for its concomitant, the federation of British North America.

One penalty he paid for living long, the loss of friends and contemporaries. Brother James died and Professor Duncan, and he found himself corresponding with the young. George Mountain's death caused him to take the train to Quebec City for the consecration of his successor. He was all but alone in his generation, but when they caught him whistling after the funeral of Mrs. Sibbald, he excused himself with the words: "With two old friends of our age, it does not matter in the least which goes first. The other must soon follow."[24]

Then in January 1863 John Beverley Robinson took gravely ill. Strachan and Grasett administered the last rites on the twenty-eighth. On the thirty-first he was dead, and Strachan was staggered by the blow. Two months later he was apologizing for his forgetfulness, for "the recent death of Sir John Beverley Robinson, my affectionate and intimate friend, has overwhelmed and distressed me."[25] Robinson had been more than a son. That tall and upright English American had been in a strange way his other self, colder, more logical, more correct, but product of his teaching for all that.

---

24   Archibald Hope Young, "John Strachan," *Queen's Quarterly*, XXXV (1928), 386.
25   SLB-SPG, p. 184, Strachan to Hawkins, 18 March 1863.

56611

Finally, through the summer of 1865, Ann's health grew rapidly worse. She was eighty, he eighty-seven. They had been married fifty-seven years. It was soon plain that this was the end. On October the eighth she too was gone. "It was my privilege during her severe illness to watch over her by night and day, which she fully appreciated,"[26] he wrote to Cronyn. It was the last such duty he was called upon to bear.

His men gave him a successor within the year. There had been attempts to do it for him already, guarded and affectionate movements by his veterans to provide the diocese with episcopal supervision while preserving Strachan's position. He was reluctant and suspicious. "Do ye wish to bury a mahn before he is dead?"[27] was one reported answer. Anxious to avoid a contest, one group memorialized him to arrange for an appointment from England. Another offered to accept Strachan's nomination. Both he declined. When it came, Toronto must face an episcopal election in the new manner and must learn by experience how to do it decently. The successful resolution was John Hillyard Cameron's in 1865. "Whenever the Bishop of the Diocese shall by writing under his hand, signify to the Synod ... that he is desirous of having a suffragan and coadjutor bishop ... such election shall be proceeded with."[28] Strachan signed, and the election came on in September 1866.

"There was," wrote Bethune later, "the development of strong and steady partialities."[29] Bethune erred, as ever, on the side of correctness. There was, in fact, an awkward stalemate. A Toronto newspaperman

---

26   PAO, Strachan Letter Book, 1862–7 (SLB 1862–7) p. 210, Strachan to Cronyn, 27 Dec. 1865.
27   Quoted in *Trinity University Review*, III (1890), 30.
28   Anglican Church of Canada, Dioceses, Toronto, *Journal of the synod of the united church of England and Ireland in the diocese of Toronto*, Thirteenth Session (Toronto: Rowsell, 1865), p. 49.
29   Bethune, *Memoir*, p. 292.

had great fun describing it in terms of a horse race, the "Race for the Mitre," between "the Bishop of Romford's white mare Cobourg Lass (aged), Mr. Trincoll's black horse Pontifex Maximus, and Mr. T. Broeck's grey horse, The Badger." "Cobourg Lass is thought by some to have a prescriptive right to the race, which would be a fitting termination to her long and honourable career on the turf."[30] For eight ballots lasting three days and nights, Bethune, Provost Whitaker, and T. Brock Fuller divided the vote, Whitaker leading with the clergy, Fuller with the laity and the evangelicals. The diocese clearly had no intention of handing itself over to Bethune. After the eighth, Whitaker requested permission of Strachan to withdraw, and the aged man had his last ecclesiastical decision to make. He accepted the provost's withdrawal. After suppressed clapping, the ninth ballot gave Bethune the necessary majority. "What was very pleasing to me," wrote Strachan, "was the affectionate deference given by the Synod to my wishes, for the man chosen was ... my old friend and pupil who has been to me a son for more than fifty years."[31] Affectionate deference might not be the best of guides in elections, but Strachan had won his man a bishopric.

The consecration presented a last difficulty. Bishop Fulford, in England on other business, applied for a Queen's mandamus to consecrate and was refused by the Colonial Secretary on the ground that the Queen's action could no longer have any meaning. The Canadian church must elect, appoint, and consecrate as it saw fit without any reference to the crown. So it was that the changeover was completed in Strachan's lifetime. He who had been appointed by government with royal letters patent and consecrated in Lambeth by Canterbury on the

---

30 Thomas Charles Patteson, *Sporting Intelligence* (Toronto: n.p., 1866), p. 4.
31 SLB 1862–7, p. 230, Strachan to Caroline Strachan, 25 Oct. 1866.

Queen's mandamus, was now called upon to consecrate in his own church his own pupil, elected by the synod he had fashioned, without reference to England.

The day chosen was January 25, 1867, the place St. James' Cathedral. A young historian described the scene. "It was interesting to see the man of sixty-seven kneeling before his old friend and master, now eighty-nine years of age, and receiving the touch of his trembling hand upon his head, the aged pair still associated together in work."[32]

John Strachan now sloughed off the cares of office. The diocese for him was in safe hands. Bethune took the confirmations and ordinations, presided over the synod and the Church Society. He intended to spend the days that were left him "preparing to meet my Redeemer."[33] Two events he watched with interest that summer. On July the first the Dominion of Canada came into being and his old Upper Canada was once more self-governing. "I trust to God," he observed, "that the measure may prosper."[34] In September, the first Pan-Anglican Conference was called to meet at Lambeth, the marshalling of all the bishops of the empire and of the United States. He was invited, and welcomed the invitation and the promise that it held. He had dreamed of it long ago. He could not go. He wrote the archbishop his apologies. "Never probably since the era of the General Councils of the Primitive Church would a more interesting and important assemblage of the Prelates of the Christian Church have been held than the meeting which is now proposed ... With these convictions, it grieves me much to say that to myself – just entering upon the ninetieth year of my age, – the gratification of joining in this most interesting meeting will be impossible. Your

32   Charles Henry Mockridge, *The Bishops of the Church of England in Canada and Newfoundland* (Toronto: F. Brown, 1896), p. 234.
33   SLB-SPG, p. 188, Strachan to Bullock.
34   SLB 1862–7, p. 243.

grace, therefore, will kindly hold me excused, on this ground, from attending; none other than this would allow me to be absent."[35] But if Strachan was prevented, Bethune must go, and at Strachan's insistence, go he did.

This was the Indian summer of the bishop. He had no regrets. He voiced no fears for the future of his church or of his diocese. The troubles that were behind were greater than any that could come again. The long series of defeats seemed to him in retrospect to be the overruling of Providence, as if his labours had been successful, if not always in the way that he had intended. He had pleasure in his house and in his garden. He went regularly to St. James' on King Street and even preached there in March. In July there came an attack which prostrated him for a while, but he was soon up again. Late in August, Bethune set off for Lambeth, leaving him well, cheery, and hopeful. Cronyn came in *en route* to the same conference and reported enjoying a long interview and spiritual communion with his lordship. "On my leaving, he invoked a blessing upon me and upon the meeting that was to take place."[36] Until October the nineteenth he could go to the cathedral, but that day he bade good-bye to the attendants, shaking the hand of each in turn. On the twenty-third he was taken seriously ill and it was obvious that he was going. A week later Dean Grasett and he received the sacrament together, and at three next morning, November 1, All Saints' Day, he was dead.

---

35 Bethune, *Memoir*, p. 294.
36 Benjamin Cronyn, "Charge to the synod of Huron," in Anglican Church of Canada, Dioceses, Huron, *Minutes of the eleventh session of the synod of the diocese of Huron* (London: Prototype printing, 1868), p. 274.

John Strachan kept copies of most of the letters that he wrote in a series of letter-books. He also kept most of those that he received together with their enclosures. As the Strachan Letter Books and the Strachan Papers in the Ontario Department of Public Records and Archives, Toronto, they remain the basis of any study of John Strachan. Strachan manuscripts may also be found in Trinity College (Toronto), the Toronto Public Library (the Scadding Papers), the Public Archives of Canada, the Archives of the United Society for the Propagation of the Gospel (London), and various private collections. As one would expect, letters to, from, or about Strachan appear among the manuscript collections of his contemporaries, the Baldwin, Cartwright, Harman, Macaulay, Ridout, and Street Papers in the Ontario Archives, the Colborne, Bagot, and Elgin Papers in the Public Archives of Canada, the Cartwright and Morris Papers of Queen's University, Kingston, to name only some. The official correspondence between the governors and the Colonial Office preserved in the Public Archives of Canada and the Public Record Office in London must also be consulted.

Again, Strachan was always writing for publication under his own name or under one of a series of pseudonyms. The Toronto Public Library has the best collection. No one has yet attempted to draw up a definitive list.

No life of Strachan has been written since Alexander Neil Bethune wrote his *Memoir of the Right Reverend John Strachan* (Toronto, 1870). George Spragge edited the *John Strachan Letter Book, 1812–1834* (Toronto, 1946) and added an admirable introduction. T. A. Reed's *History of the University of Trinity College, Toronto* (Toronto,

1952) includes an essay on "The Founder." No history of the period ignores him. John Moir in *Church and State in Canada West* (Toronto, 1959) investigates problems raised by the attempt at an establishment. Alan Wilson, *The Clergy Reserves of Upper Canada* (Toronto, 1968), makes sense out of that tangled subject. Judson Purdy's University of Toronto thesis "John Strachan and Education in Canada," available on microfilm, explores one side of Strachan's life. The most useful general works on the period are Gerald Craig's *Upper Canada: The Formative Years, 1784–1841* (Toronto, 1963), and J. M. S. Careless's *The Union of the Canadas: The Growth of Canadian Institutions, 1841–1857* (Toronto, 1967). Paul Cornell's *The Alignment of Political Groups in Canada, 1841–1867* (Toronto, 1962) illustrates and illuminates the complexity of politics in the united province.

Index